The Marble in the Water

♦

The Marble

Essays on contemporary writers

BOSTON 1980

in the Water

of fiction for children and young adults

by David Rees

THE HORN BOOK, INC.

Printed in the United States of America
Library of Congress Cataloging in Publication Data

Rees, David, 1936 —
   The marble in the water.

     Includes bibliographies.
     Includes index.
     1. Children's stories, American — History and criticism — Addresses, essays, lectures. 2. Children's stories, English — History and criticism — Addresses, essays, lectures. I. Title.
PN1009.AIR42   823'.912'099282   80-16623
ISBN 0-87675-280-6
ISBN 0-87675-281-4 (pbk.)

In memory of Sidney Robbins

Great works of imaginative literature . . .
are hospitals where we heal . . .
when they are evil works they are
battlefields where we get injured.

— Ted Hughes
Myth and Education

Perhaps books can help, just a little

— Penelope Lively
Children and Memory

Acknowledgments

◆

MY THANKS are due to Paul and Ethel Heins for their enthusiasm and encouragement; to the late Sidney Robbins for bullying me into my first attempt at criticism, the essay on Philippa Pearce — and for much more; to Penelope Lively; to Penelope Farmer; to Joanna Goldsworthy; to Janet Schulman; to Kim Stephens for suggesting parallels between E. B. White and Doris Buchanan Smith; to Dorothy and Tony Steer; and to Geoff Fox for reading the manuscript. Six of these essays originally appeared, in slightly different form, in other publications. The essays on Philippa Pearce and Jill Chaney were first published in *Children's literature in education*, in March 1971 and in Summer 1977 respectively. Four appeared in *The Horn Book Magazine* — on Penelope Lively in February 1975; on Penelope Farmer in October 1976; on E. L. Konigsburg in February 1978 and on Alan Garner in June 1979. The introduction to the essay on Mildred Taylor appeared in an essay on James Vance Marshall in *Children's literature in education* in Summer 1980.

Contents

◆

Introduction

◆

THE PURPOSES of this collection of essays are several. In choosing to discuss the work of eight English and ten American authors, I hope to explore some of the likenesses and the major differences in fiction for children and young adults of both our nations. I am not trying to suggest that one tradition is superior to the other; it seems to me that between us we have a particularly rich heritage, one that is probably more varied than the children's literature of any other language.

I am inclined to agree, however, with Sheila Egoff, who, in the April 1970 issue of *The Horn Book Magazine*, argued that young people in modern American books for children and young adults are "the unhappiest, most upset, distressed, suspicious, alienated, introspective generation the world has ever known" and that "most of the time they are smothered in their own unhappiness and for fairly ordinary reasons." I would only add that her remarks are equally true of youngsters in most contemporary British children's books as well. I particularly value, therefore, the work of a writer such as Ursula Le Guin who appears to be putting forward a quite opposite point of view. The young, in my opinion, are in real life no happier nor unhappier than were their predecessors, and if, in literature about them, they are portrayed otherwise, the reason is likely to be that the authors are working out their own dissatisfactions, rearranging in fictional terms the problems of their own childhood and adolescence. There is nothing wrong with that; the writer of a novel for children has, of necessity, to be vividly in touch with his own roots and formative years, and unhappiness is probably a greater spur to creativity than is total self-fulfillment. A large number of our children's writers spent their early lives in the period of the Second World War, and suffered — as well as benefited — from the damage to roots that new opportunities in education brought. The result, however, of reading a great deal of recent fiction for children is that we are presented with a view of the young that is perhaps a little lopsided.

I hope these essays point out some of the qualities of American literature that are of particular appeal to the young in England, and which authors are, or are not, successful here; but I cannot, for obvious reasons, make a similar assessment of the reception of British children's books in the United States. An American has to do that. I can, of course, discuss the characteristics of the current scene in Britain, which is something that gives no one any grounds for complacency. Jill Paton Walsh said recently that had she started writing ten years later than she did, she would have found it much harder to get herself established. She is absolutely right. It is not so much because the market is now overcrowded with new practitioners of the first rank, but because enthusiasm for, and interest in, children's fiction has declined during the nineteen-seventies. Looking back, the late sixties now seem like a golden age, particularly the years 1967-1968, during which were published *A Wizard of Earthsea; The Owl Service; The Children of the House; How Many Miles to Babylon?; The Stone-Faced Boy; From the Mixed-up Files of Mrs. Basil E. Frankweiler; Jennifer, Hecate, Macbeth, William McKinley, and Me, Elizabeth; The Pigman;* and *The Iron Giant*, to name but a few of the more obvious titles; and they were widely reviewed, and eagerly read and discussed, not only by children but by adults discovering that major writing talents were busily engaged with novels for the young. Ten years later indifference is all too common. Apart from the specialist journals, the British and American press mostly ignore our important book awards; review space in Britain and America has shrunk to a pathetic all-time low; critics relive the achievements of the sixties instead of assessing new fiction; each year fewer books are bought and read. Even the specialist journals cannot escape some of the blame; *Books for Your Children*, which appears twice-yearly in England, consistently gives a second, a third, a fourth opinion of some ten-year-old work of an established writer rather than devoting sufficient space to new novels. Therefore another purpose of this collection of essays is to call attention to certain good — indeed very good — writers whose work is being unjustifiably ignored, and also to point out that some of our more famous authors do not always match up to the praise that is lavished upon them.

Serious academic criticism of literature for children is not an art that is widely practised in England, and in most English universities it is likely to be regarded as a time-wasting, frivolous pastime. In this respect, we have a lot to learn from the kind of criticism which appears in the United States. Although it is regrettable that in England there are very few important books on the subject, we are not plagued by conflicting schools of thought; there is no prevailing orthodoxy in criticism of children's fiction to which one must either subscribe or be excommunicated from. This gives us great freedom, so I make no apology for choosing to write on an author as undervalued as Rodie Sudbery and not once, in the course of this book, mentioning William Mayne; just as I feel that it is perfectly proper to question the supposed excellence of writers like Alan Garner and Jill Paton Walsh, to try and put Judy Blume in her place, and to state that we consistently undervalue the work of others, such as Penelope Farmer and Paula Fox.

I hope, above all, that in both England and America, we will soon begin to relish the considerable differences between our two cultural traditions, and stop grumbling that E. L. Konigsburg is "too American" or that Philippa Pearce is "too British." An Americanized *Tom's Midnight Garden* and an Anglicized *Mrs. Frankweiler* are surely quite unthinkable ideas. *Vive la difference!*

The Marble
in the Water

♦

PENELOPE FARMER

MOST WRITERS of fiction for children, when asked what kind of audience they are writing for, usually reply that they are writing primarily for themselves and if the book turns out to be a children's book — well, that is, perhaps, accidental. The statement, I feel, is not always totally honest. With Penelope Farmer, however, it is probably more honest than with most writers. Her achievement seems to be a number of successful books for children arising from preoccupations which are strongly personal, themes and ideas that might easily have found voice in novels written for an adult audience. These preoccupations recur, sometimes obsessively: The wish every one has had at least once in his life to be able to fly, for example, is the main theme of both *The Summer Birds* and *Emma in Winter* and also of her picture book *Daedalus and Icarus;* it reappears, disguised as a desire to swim underwater like a fish, in *William and Mary*. Obviously it would be possible to use such a theme in a totally adult way, to use it as a means of expressing some kind of liberation from the body, perhaps sexual; but in Penelope Farmer's books the theme is simply the child's wish to fly like a bird come true.

Penelope Farmer's books come under the convenient label of *fantasy*, and this is a label that may unfortunately suggest that a writer is unable to, or chooses not to, write realistic fiction. However, in most fantasies the real world is usually still there as a stark contrast; it comments on the fantasy, brings it more clearly into focus, offers relief or causes consternation as the case may be to the protagonists, just as the fantasy has a similar job to do on the real world. Few good writers of fantasy ignore the everyday outside world — one has only to think of Catherine Storr, Philippa Pearce, Lucy Boston — and Penelope Farmer, too, is just as much at home in writing about the interior of chemists' shops, the smell of school kitchens, or the relationships between children and adults as she is about cupboards that turn matchboxes into fir trees or the inside of a whale that seems to be a plush hotel. Three of her books — *The Dragonfly Summer, Saturday Shillings,* and *The Seagull* — dispense with fantasy altogether, and they are good examples of how well she can write in a medium with which we do not normally associate her. In fact, it could be argued that *Charlotte Sometimes*, probably her most widely read novel, is not a fantasy at all, for the only nonrealistic device in this book is the bed that turns Charlotte into Clare who lived forty years before; the world of the last few months of the 1914-1918 war is just as realistic as Charlotte's boarding school in the present. It is the only book of hers in which dream sequences or events that are completely fantastic are not employed in the parts of the book which are supposedly fantasy.

In four of the seven novels — five, if we include the 1918 passages of *Charlotte Sometimes* — two different worlds are sharply contrasted, the everyday and the extraordinary. The extraordinary involves only the child protagonists, and their problems usually occur because the dream world has its good and its evil just as the real has; but the children can never turn for help to the real world — the safe security of home and parents — because they will either not be believed or the trouble will be worse if they do. Hugh, Anna, and Jean, for example, in *A Castle of Bone*, have to manage on their own. The magic cupboard has turned adolescent Penn into a baby.

2 •

To ask his parents or Hugh's parents for assistance would obviously be impossible; the recriminations and the anguish would be extreme and would not help to turn Penn back into his normal self. In any case it is the children's own fault; Penn was shut in the cupboard as a result of a violent quarrel between him and his sister, which Hugh and Jean did nothing to stop – a scene which is a microcosm of what is fundamentally at fault in the relationships among the four. It is only right that the children extricate themselves unassisted from the difficulties they have made; only by doing so can they achieve a more mature relationship with each other.

The dream sequences in *Emma in Winter* have a similar function. They become, on the whole, increasingly unpleasant and are mirrored in the everyday world by the mounting tensions in the village caused by the unusually lengthy period of frost and snow. At first the dreams are delightful, the sense of liberation and happiness caused by the ability to fly being predominant, just as Emma and her friends take delight in the snow, which turns the ordinary landscape into a fairy-tale paradise and pleasantly disrupts the tedium of the day-to-day rhythm of their lives:

> But outside the window the snow fell soundless, flickering. It had buried the garden almost completely and turned the lawn into a wide, white plain. It had blurred the long smooth line of the beech trees; their separate branches were all swollen with snow like the thickest summer foliage. At one side of the lawn the steep bank bumped up the snow like the knees of a giant beneath an eiderdown. But on the other side, where the drive should have been, the white plain swept on quite smooth to the group of round white swellings that were usually the dark rhododendron bushes. And still the snow was falling, swaying past the window pane where Emma pressed her nose, holding her almost spellbound, watching it fall.

◆ 3

But something is wrong: Emma's selfishness and unmerited sense of superiority cause a great deal of unhappiness, particularly to the clumsy fat boy, Bobby Fumpkins, who adores her, and also to her teacher, Miss Hallibutt, who overlooks her faults too easily because Emma has brains. It is only by learning to compromise, by growing up in these two relationships in the dreams that Emma is able to mature in her actual relationships with these people, and the dreams — now nightmares — can stop.

Poor Charlotte is a different case. It cannot be argued that she is responsible for what happens to her, that she in any way deserves it; nor can it be said that the book, like *Emma in Winter* and *A Castle of Bone*, is about growing up, growing awareness, maturing relationships. In fact, with the exception of *Year King*, it seems to be much more of an adult book than any other novel by Penelope Farmer. This may seem to be an odd judgment, when it is remembered that it has sold extremely well in the Puffin edition, has been serialized on children's television, and that *A Castle of Bone* is often unfavorably commented on — by adults — as being either too adult, sinister, or even evil, whereas no one has said this of *Charlotte Sometimes*. What disturbs many people about *A Castle of Bone* — adults again, not children — is that Penn is shut in the cupboard, more or less deliberately, by his sister. However, it seems a common enough action to children, a sister shutting her brother in a cupboard, an everyday family event, even. The prevailing mood of *Charlotte Sometimes* is, perhaps, not part of the child's world. Whatever may happen in *Emma in Winter* and *A Castle of Bone*, they remain in essence happy books, even joyous at times. Hugh's pleasure in his own adolescence, the shifts of his moods, the achieving of new experiences are, for instance, very positive, as is the sequence where Bobby Fumpkins helps his father dig in the snow. Both books are often comic; the passage where Molly Scobb thinks she has given Emma her come-uppance is a very amusing and realistic piece of observation, and Hugh's attempts to buy baby food and nipples have a zany, almost clown-like quality:

> Why shouldn't he buy a teat if he wanted to, why should he be obliged to explain? So he handed over his money and emerged from the shop almost dizzy with relief at having obtained it safely, so dizzy indeed that he forgot the tin of milk and had to turn back to the supermarket where he waited behind a woman buying a dozen tins of pilchards, for her children, it appeared, not cats. (If it had been for her cats, she explained to Hugh, she would have bought the kind without tomato sauce.)

Such moments are absent from *Charlotte Sometimes*, the atmosphere of which is low key, one of depression. Its most memorable passages are poignant or resigned or concerned with absence, loss, or death in action during the war:

> They had to sit in the big classroom, doing preparation in charge of Miss Wilkin, whose fiancé had been killed at the front the week before. Though neat as ever, she looked bedraggled somehow, today a little shrunk, her clothes not quite so tight on her as before. She had pen and paper but did not write; she twisted her ring continually, but did not look at it.

Its theme is not so much maturing relationships, but identity. This is a perfectly proper theme for children's fiction, of course, for why am I I, and not John Smith or Julie Bloggs, is a normal preoccupation of the thoughtful child. But the book goes further than this. Charlotte begins to wonder, with increasing dismay, if she really is Charlotte; perhaps she has turned into Clare, rather than just substituted for her. This may be an adult fear — the fear of not being everything you and other people have always said you are, the realization that you may be someone totally different, that maybe there isn't such a thing as yourself at all, only a series of different images other people have of you that don't add up to anything coherent.

A key passage in *Charlotte Sometimes* occurs in chapter sixteen:

> But when she put her fingers into the water and pulled a marble out, it was small by comparison with those still in the glass, and unimportant, too. It was like the difference between what you long 'for and what you find — the difference, for instance, between Arthur's image of war and his experience of it. It was like other times, her own and Miss Agnes's proper childhood times that seemed so near to her memory and yet so far away. It was like everything that made you ache because in one sense it was so close and in another unobtainable.

One might find similar paragraphs in other children's books that deal with the idea of illusion and reality; one thinks, for example, of Granny Fitch's remark in Philippa Pearce's *A Dog So Small* — " 'People get their heart's desire . . . and then they have to begin to learn how to live with it.' " But the context of this passage in *Charlotte Sometimes* makes it particularly heartfelt, coming just after the pathetic Agnes — doomed for the rest of her unfulfilled life to a sad spinsterhood — reveals to Charlotte that the image of her brother dying heroically in battle, an image her parents believe in and which she tries hard to subscribe to, is very far from the truth. It seems to have a wholly adult feeling about it, which is added to by Charlotte's inability to cope with the adult reactions and emotions of Agnes.

Inability to cope with adult situations: This might be said of Charlotte's response to her predicament as a whole. In the other books the children grapple with problems, often with zest, and either overcome them or come to terms with them. Charlotte does not; she struggles only feebly with the situation, just keeping her head above water. It is significant, perhaps, that it is not she who organizes her return to her own world, but Emily.

None of this is a criticism of *Charlotte Sometimes*; the book is none the worse for breaking the conventional bounds of the children's novel. It is probably Penelope Farmer's finest novel — complex, taut, not a word wrong — and it thoroughly deserves the popularity it has attained. *A Castle of Bone* ought to be her best book; its central idea is more strikingly original, the characters more vivid and varied, its potential, both serious and comic, greater. But it remains a flawed achievement. In her lecture "Patterns on a Wall" Penelope Farmer says that the castle of bone image, taken from a Welsh triad, was

> ...not relevant to the book I was proposing to write; nor could I see any way of making it so. But the image took over, took me and the book over, wormed its way into the plot till it was central.

It is central enough at the end; indeed, the denouement could not work without it, but in most of the book it isn't central. Hugh's dreams do not seem to fit into the rest of the story; there is a strong temptation to skip over them and return to what is happening to the children and to the cupboard. For most of the time the castle image does not seem apposite or even very interesting, and one might say that it is a pity that "the image took over, took . . . the book over," as the author reveals, rather than the other way round.

It is difficult to find anything wrong with either *Emma in Winter* or *William and Mary*, but neither of these books compete with *Charlotte Sometimes*, because they do not aim at anything quite so rich or profound. It is perhaps appropriate here to say something about *William and Mary* and Penelope Farmer's first two novels, *The Summer Birds* and *The Magic Stone*, and why they do not measure up to *Charlotte Sometimes*. *William and Mary* comes after *Charlotte Sometimes* and *A Castle of Bone*, but it seems in many ways a return to an earlier manner, the simpler world of *Emma in Winter*. It has the same kind of central relationship, a boy and a girl whose friendship helps at least one of the two to mature, and the fantasy, juxtaposed in self-contained sections with the everyday world, has the same episodic nature as Emma's dreams. The real world as in *Charlotte Sometimes* is a boarding school; only now it is the holidays; Mary is the headmaster's daughter, alone in a vast empty building, alone even during term time in being the only girl among hundreds of boys. She has some of Charlotte's sense of being apart from everyone else. The bleakness of a seaside resort out of season echoes Mary's loneliness:

> They walked up as far as the pier and peered through its locked and rusty gates at the dilapidated kiosks and seats lacking most of their slats. The boards looked rotten, stained different shades of grey and brown, and several were splintered as if feet had gone through them. There were traces of posters on the kiosks, shadows of bright colours, and below the sea complained with echoing, melancholy sounds that made Mary melancholy too for a moment, perhaps William also.

But William has the shell, the talisman — that most popular of devices in fantasies, like C. S. Lewis's wardrobe or Philippa Pearce's clock which strikes thirteen or Dr. Who's telephone box — which transports the children to another world, in this case under the sea to Atlantis or Dunwich or the depths of the Pacific Ocean. William's search for the other half of the shell is mirrored in real life by his wish to bring his separated parents together. The book is perfectly done; the relationship between William and Mary is full of insights, the fantasy comic or bewildering or sinister (one is constantly aware in this book of fishes' teeth and claws and the murky depths of the sea).

> "Then what are those things in your mouth?" asked Mary.
> "Ah, that is a very neat, very satisfactory arrange-

ment," said the whale. "That is a means of filtering my food, so I take in only what is wholesome and appropriate, the smallest, most innocuous of animals. But that need not concern you in any case. What I have to offer you is board and lodgings. The bedrooms, I assure you, are clean and comfortable, with all conveniences and running water, naturally."

Nevertheless, after the previous two books it seems slight, the kind of novel which the author knows she can do well because by now she is well practiced in this kind of thing, but it does not seem to be one that has engaged the whole of her attention nor the whole of the imaginative power that the preceding two have revealed.

The Summer Birds and The Magic Stone are essentially apprentice books in which the author is trying to make up her mind what kind of book she can write. This is especially true of The Magic Stone, most of which is a realistic analysis (if somewhat labored) of the relationship between two adolescent girls, whose antagonism – they come from quite different social classes — is muted by their discovery of a stone which seems to have magical powers and which may have had some connection with King Arthur. It has some striking passages, particularly its opening description of Caroline watching Alice who is bringing in the washing; trying to cope with her younger brother, she is full of annoyance that Caroline can see her. But the fantasy is very obscure. What powers does the stone have? Is it King Arthur's? Neither the characters, nor the author, it seems, are at all sure.

The Summer Birds is the better book. Flying is the central theme, and the pleasures and sensations of this impossible human activity are effectively explored. For a first novel it is fine; nothing much wrong with it anywhere except for some awkward stylistic lapses, but it remains a small thing, for the relationships, though perfectly convincing, are not shown in any depth. It is the

◆ 9

book of Penelope Farmer's which is the least adult, the one that is contained most entirely in a child's world.

One might well ask why a children's book shouldn't be contained entirely in a child's world. Many people, C. S. Lewis included, have said that a really good children's book ought to appeal to adults as much as to children, for then it is not limited by saying something to only a certain group of readers; it is simply a good book. And this appeal is what *Charlotte Sometimes* has that *The Summer Birds* has not; it enhances the perceptions of all of us, helps our imaginations, whether child or adult, to grow in the most pleasurable of ways. And that is what reading and writing should be about. This is said by Penelope Farmer herself in "Patterns on a Wall":

> I'm coming increasingly to wonder whether I actually write children's books and certainly feel I won't continue to do so much longer.

Year King, her most recent novel, is a good illustration of this remark. It is longer than any of her previous books; its preoccupations are larger, its style more analytical and compressed. It is published in Great Britain and the United States as a book for young people, and it has been said that it isn't a children's book at all; but it seems to me that, complex though the book is, this objection is not relevant, for it can certainly be appreciated by the intelligent adolescent, and its themes — first love, identity, discovering one's potential as a person — are no different from those of the average teenage novel. Its difficulties are those of manner, not matter; but they are small compared, for instance, with the obscurities of Alan Garner's *Red Shift*, also published on a children's list. The central characters are identical twins, boys, aged nineteen. Lan has a huge inferiority complex with regard to his brother; Lew is academically brilliant, more successful with girls, first-rate at sport. We observe the action through Lan's eyes: compared with his brother he is in

every way clumsy. At crucial moments of excitement or
danger he finds that he is no longer inside his own body,
but has turned into Lew: when he is surfing, or on the
point of going to bed with his girl friend, or riding a
motor-bike rather carelessly round a sharp bend he becomes Lew, who is actually miles away at a lecture in
Cambridge or dangling on the end of a rope on a rock-
face. Lew, he realizes, is trying to kill him.

This pushes the problems of identity raised in *Charlotte Sometimes* still further: the central question of *Year
King* is, who am I? What do I want to be? And have I
the courage to achieve it, to resist the pressures that will
stop me? Yet the book has strengths apart from its plot
and the fascinating questions it asks. The evocation of
landscape — the Brendon Hills in Somerset — is superbly
done; "up there, on the bank, he thought: I am a colossus
— I bestride the world." The opening paragraph says:

> It is two countries: very bleak on the uplands in winter,
> the no less so for being obviously well tilled and fertile;
> much more outwardly fecund and welcoming lower
> down, as it descends towards the sea. You reach one
> from the other, move from austerity to softness, to the
> world of church instead of chapel, in the blink of an eye.

It is the same landscape as that of Penelope Lively's
Going Back, the same village, but observed quite differently, though Penelope Lively also sees "two countries":

> a landscape of fields and hills and lanes, tranquil and
> harmless — but then it was the unpredictable, into which
> one did not go.

Few novels suggest as sharply as *Year King* does the
power of place, and how, under the influence of over-
whelming events — Lan's first real love affair as well as
his struggle with Lew — landscape and emotion become
inextricably woven. And not always pleasantly; the destructive power of jealousy is important here, for the girl

is sleeping with both brothers, and Lan's discovery of this fact nearly ruins everything.

Details of existence in a remote rural community come vividly alive: the farming, the inevitable Exmoor stag-hunting, a village hall dance. Less succeessful perhaps, because it's too vague, is the attempt to give the narrative mythological overtones; the story itself has the strength of myth without the need to hint at parallels.

What is the sum of her achievement so far? Her use of fantasy is probably more personal in origin than that employed by most children's writers yet it has been successfully manipulated to produce seven books that deal with not personal, but universal, problems and ideas in a way that they could not be dealt with in more realistic books. Penelope Farmer writes in "Jorinda and Jorindel and Other Stories":

> I doubt if you could find any piece of realistic fiction for adolescents that says a quarter as much about adolescence as Alan Garner's *The Owl Service*.

The same claim is so true of certain aspects of childhood and adolescence in her own novels that she should be more widely known and read than she is. She deserves much greater recognition; she's one of the finest of English authors and the most underrated of them all.

References

PENELOPE FARMER

The Summer Birds Chatto 1962; Harcourt 1962
The Magic Stone Chatto 1965; Harcourt 1965
Saturday Shillings Hamish Hamilton 1965
The Seagull Hamish Hamilton 1966; Harcourt 1966
Emma in Winter Chatto 1966; Harcourt 1966
Charlotte Sometimes Chatto 1969; Harcourt 1969
Daedalus and Icarus Collins, London, 1971; Harcourt 1971

The Dragonfly Summer Hamish Hamilton 1971
A Castle of Bone Chatto 1972; Atheneum 1972
William and Mary Chatto 1974; Atheneum 1974
Year King Chatto 1977; Atheneum 1977
"Patterns on a Wall" *The Horn Book Magazine*,
October 1974
"Jorinda and Jorindel and Other Stories" *Children's
literature in education* March 1972

PHILIPPA PEARCE
A Dog So Small Constable 1962; Lippincott 1963

ALAN GARNER
The Owl Service Collins, London, 1967; Walck 1968
Red Shift Collins, London, 1973; Macmillan, New York,
1973

PENELOPE LIVELY
Going Back Heinemann 1975; Dutton 1975

Your Arcane Novelist

◆

E. L. KONIGSBURG

AIDAN CHAMBERS, in the October 1976 *Horn Book*, writes interestingly about some of the differences between English and American writers of children's books and about why some American writers are more popular with English children than British authors are with young readers in the United States. He speaks of the "breezy uninhibitedness of American writing," its sense of insecurity with which the adolescent in particular may find it easy to identify, its lack of class-based assumptions and culturally narrow references. He quotes the opening of Paul Zindel's *The Pigman* to support his view and says, quite rightly, that it is very popular with English children. I have no quarrel with his assessment of the strength of much modern American writing that finds its way into British homes and schools, but he misses one important point, which is illustrated by the opening words of *The Pigman*. I am referring to a question of style, of voice. Zindel's writing reflects the American adult's generalized view of the all-American teenager: edgy, fluent, certainly uninhibited, and "with it." But the voice lacks individuality. It is the same voice that occurs in many — perhaps too many — contemporary American authors, the voice of Holden Caulfield. The influence of Salinger on the present generation of American writers for children seems profound, all-pervasive. Maybe English readers miss subtlety and nuance, just as Americans may miss the differences in style that seem obvious to the

English among, say, Rosemary Sutcliff and Lucy Boston and Philippa Pearce (all very English novelists).

Three Americans that, to the British reader at least, stand apart from their fellow novelists are Ursula Le Guin, Paula Fox, and Elaine Konigsburg, and a major reason for their popularity here is their distinctness of voice. There's no mistaking them for anybody else, and with distinctness of voice goes distinctness of preoccupation; the material they choose to write about is peculiarly their own, and when they do venture into areas that seem to be the common property of most American children's writers, as in Konigsburg's (*George*) or Le Guin's *Very Far Away from Anywhere Else*, their methods and their attitudes are markedly different from and more successful than — from a British point of view at least — those of their contemporaries.

Not that Elaine Konigsburg crosses the Atlantic all that easily. Two of her books are not published in England; her editors there feel that *About the B'nai Bagels* and *Altogether One at a Time* are almost impenetrably American to the English reader. This fact, in a sense, testifies to the great variety in her books, for the two historical novels, *A Proud Taste for Scarlet and Miniver* and *The Second Mrs. Giaconda*, have nothing at all American about them, apart from the occasional use of a word like "guy" instead of "man." Interestingly, her books which are more specifically American and which are better than her two historical novels — particularly *From the Mixed-up Files of Mrs. Basil E. Frankweiler* — have been the most successful in England. This fact bears out Aidan Chambers's point about the popularity of American children's fiction in this country.

(*George*) is probably Elaine Konigsburg's finest achievement so far, though it is less well-known in England than *From the Mixed-up Files of Mrs. Basil E. Frankweiler*. The bald outline of (*George*) is, at first sight, enough to make many English readers groan: a book about the highly precocious schizophrenic elder son of a broken marriage, who attends a school for especially gifted children, whose mother is being courted by the man who teaches the boy his favorite subject, chemistry. Not another psychological case study turned into fiction, not another neurotic American child! The book is, of course, a delight. The skill with which Mrs. Konigsburg turns this apparently formidable material into a light-hearted, genuinely comic novel is immense. Its success lies in the author's decision to treat the darker, more socially unacceptable side of the split personality (the Mr. Hyde as opposed to the Dr. Jekyll) as a real, separate person who lives inside Ben and also in her belief, completely convincing to the reader, that Ben has to find ways by himself to marry the two parts of his personality rather than be further damaged by unhelpful efforts on the part of certain adults, such as his father's second wife. The right sort of adults are, nevertheless, shown to be of some importance: Mr. Berkowitz, the chemistry teacher, is one of these. He has wisdom and an ability to love — a willingness to ignore the superficial unattractiveness of the Carr family, with its untidy house and the irritating rudeness of the younger brother, and value the real qualities of Ben, Howard, and Mrs. Carr. He is seen in stark contrast to the second Mrs. Carr, whose preoccupations with cleanliness, educational toys, and doing what is fashionably correct destroy any ability she may have had to respond unselfishly and naturally to other people; she's the kind of person who makes young people neurotic, a destructive woman, not a healer:

> "You can reverse the charges," she said. Ben was silent. "I know that this is all something of a surprise to you, Ben. Finding out that you are going home and that you are a schizo when you weren't expecting that either. Schizo is what we call schizophrenic in psych.

We are so very concerned, your dad and I, that we
don't think there's a moment to lose. And we think it
will be better for you and for Frederica."

"Is it contagious?"

"No, Ben, but we want Frederica to experience
only the most normal things. We don't think that it is
fair to her to expose her to having to make compromises
with her normal growth pattern."

"I get it," said Ben.

(*George*), like so many really good modern children's
books, deals with the theme *who am I?* Questions of
identity — "What kind of person can I become?" — are
fundamentally serious ideas, even if the surface is comedy,
and they are present in nearly all Elaine Konigsburg's
stories, though less obviously than in (*George*). If *From
the Mixed-up Files of Mrs. Basil E. Frankweiler* is a less
successful novel, it is probably because the idea is buried
too deep below the surface. There are some awkward
questions that remain unanswered in this book. Why, for
instance, do the children seem to think so little about
what their parents and brothers are feeling? They are
not, surely, as callous and unthinking as they appear to be.
If we are not told enough about this, it is because the
author has become too preoccupied with the highly in-
genious and thoroughly entertaining idea of where Claudia
and Jamie run away to — the Metropolitan Museum of
Art in New York, where they can sleep in the bed in
which Amy Robsart was murdered, bathe in a fountain,
store their belongings in a Roman sarcophagus, and even
continue their education by studying Renaissance art. The
comedy of the book is marvelous, the dialogue sparkling:
Jamie finds a picture of Michelangelo in an art book and
Claudia says —

> "There's his broken nose." She pointed to the nose
> in the picture. "He got in a fight and had his nose   ♦ 17
> broken when he was a teenager."

"Was he a juvenile delinquent? Maybe they have his fingerprints on file."

"No, silly," Claudia said. "He was a hot-tempered genius. Did you know he was famous even when he was alive?"

"Is that so? I thought that artists don't become famous until after they're dead. Like mummies."

But the book needs a story, and the story we are given, the children's attempts to find out whether the statue of an angel was carved by Michelangelo, is thin. It inevitably leads — because the author feels the mystery must be solved — to the rather unlikely figure of Mrs. Frankweiler, a kind of fairy godmother and *deus ex machina*, who sorts out the problem and the children, whereas the children should have sorted out both the problem and themselves on their own. That would have required a different story line, of course, one that would have nothing to do with discovering whether Michelangelo carved the angel or not. The statue nearly places the book in a different and less reputable genre: Children beat the experts. But Elaine Konigsburg, being wise enough to know that children on the whole don't, and perhaps shouldn't, beat the experts, is forced into the Mrs. Frankweiler device which, though more acceptable in some ways, is far too contrived.

She scored a unique triumph in 1968 by winning the Newbery Medal for *From the Mixed-up Files of Mrs. Basil E. Frankweiler* and having her first novel, *Jennifer, Hecate, Macbeth, William McKinley, and Me, Elizabeth* named an honor book; but with hindsight the order of merit now appears curious, for the earlier book is by far the more satisfying and better resolved of the two. Its central character Elizabeth, like Ben in (*George*) is a child who has difficulty making friends; the girl she finds interesting is the strange loner Jennifer, an intelligent and imaginative person whose influence is so powerful that she succeeds in convincing Elizabeth — and the reader —

that she is a witch. The denouement of the story is extremely subtle; only when Elizabeth, for the first time, refuses to obey one of Jennifer's commands — to put a live toad in a bubbling cauldron — is it possible for her to see that the whole thing has been an elaborate hoax; and from that moment the two girls are on an equal footing and become real friends. The book neatly illustrates the point that friendship is limited, frustrating even, when one of the two people is domineering and the other meekly subservient; much greater satisfaction is possible when the false relationship is broken. The observation of incidentals throughout the book is sharp and extremely witty. The description, for instance, of the worst kind of school play — a sort of class-written nativity — makes the reader wonder why on earth our schools waste energy on such futile pursuits. It was a long play, we're told. "It had to be long so that all sixty kids could get a chance to act. Our school was democratic about Christmas."

> It was a long rehearsal. All the teachers except Mrs. Stuyvestant took coffee breaks. Everyone had to be prompted. Everyone stood in the wrong places. Mrs. Stuyvestant would bounce up on stage and move the people around. She made chalk marks on the stage where they were to stand. By the end of that first rehearsal the floor looked like our classroom blackboard just after Miss Hazen explained long division by the New Math.

Other targets for satire are a pair of elderly health-food faddists and Cynthia, the child who is everything so many adults adore but who is shown to be mean and two-faced. The world is full of Cynthias, children who quickly learn to play the tricks adults demand and in so doing lose their ability to be themselves.

In (George) the idea is developed further through the characters of William and Cheryl — a rather more sinister version because they are so much older; and they, too, manipulate adults by presenting a superficially nice, conformist image in order to engage in some fairly evil pastimes, such as the manufacture of LSD. Another character of this kind is Salai in *The Second Mrs. Giaconda,* and he is given a quite different twist; though he, too, knows how to smile in order to conceal, what potential he has for evil is checked and rendered harmless by Leonardo's consistently treating him with kindness. It is the nonconformist child who may find life difficult but who clings to his integrity that Elaine Konigsburg shows in most of her books as likely to make the mature, whole adult — Ben, Claudia, Jennifer, Elizabeth, and Winston in *Father's Arcane Daughter* — and we share her considerable dislike for parents who force their children into patterns of behavior that damage or destroy that integrity, such as the Carmichaels or the second Mrs. Carr.

Andy, in *The Dragon in the Ghetto Caper,* is a child whose integrity has been damaged by his well-to-do status-seeking parents. He lacks "dragons": the more spontaneous, uninhibited aspects of life — a symbol which seems a bit labored as it sticks rather too obviously through the text at times. He retreats into an absurd fantasy world in which he imagines he is a famous detective. From this he is rescued by an extremely unconventional woman, Edie Yakots, the sort of eccentric we find more commonly in the novels of Paula Fox; Edie shows him that his life is very limited and that, although he is not to blame for this, he is making it much worse for himself than he needs to. The final eye-opener for Andy comes when he thinks he's caught some crooks trying to steal his sister's wedding presents; in fact, they are detectives who think he is master-minding a gambling racket. The mistakes are sorted out and the story ends with Andy taking a long hard look at himself. The material of this book may not sound very original, but what distinguishes it from others of its type is the clarity of the writing, the author's eye for vivid detail, and her sense of fun. Elaine Konigsburg is among the wittiest of all

American writers for children. "Nice ghetto you've got here," Andy says to a black woman, not understanding the implications of the word. Edie, waving to Andy, looks like "an antenna in a high wind." The ethos of the school he attends, and its effects on him, are nicely summed up: "The policy there was not to *make* Andrew go to music but to make him *want* to go. They never succeeded." There are some amusing moments when Edie decides that the best way to handle this strange boy is to do exactly what he says, so that he'll see that the image he has of himself is ridiculous:

> He got to the car a few strides ahead of her, opened the back door, jumped in, slouched down all the way to the floor and said, "Okay, Yakots, let's move it, and don't spare the treads."
>
> Edie stepped on the gas and pulled away with a screech of rubber. Every teacher, K through six, looked up. Two of them took down the color and make of the car, and one made a note of the license plate number.
>
> "What's the matter, Andy?" Andy didn't answer. He had about 200 degrees to go through before he was cool.

The humor, as here, often consists of using cliché in a new context, so that something familiar is looked at satirically and shown as threadbare; the cliché is itself mocked. Economy of phrase, humor on more than one level: these qualities help to make Elaine Konigsburg's voice so distinctive.

The two historical stories — *A Proud Taste for Scarlet and Miniver* and *The Second Mrs. Giaconda* as well as the most recent novel, *Father's Arcane Daughter* — are rather disappointing. The author's usual skills are there: her ability to make a surprise ending sound totally right, her wit, the general flow of her narrative, and her sharp and clever characterization — but something is missing. The historical stories are accurate in their facts or in such facts as are known; and what is guesswork — for example, why Leonardo painted a portrait of the second wife of an obscure Florentine merchant rather than that of Isabella Gonzaga, Duchess of Mantua, who would have paid him considerably more than Signor Giaconda could afford — is given interesting and plausible explanation. What seems to be wrong is that the stories are not sufficiently exciting in themselves; the reader feels less of an urge than, for instance, with (*George*) to keep turning the pages to find out what happens next. Also, the author does not seem to have forged a convincing enough mode of speech for her historical characters. Of course they cannot be allowed to converse in the manner of American teenagers nor in the dialect and vocabulary of medieval England or sixteenth-century Florence; but the language that she uses — modern speech, devoid of the slang that would place it too precisely — though a reasonable instrument, does not sound fluent and natural. People speak too much like the characters in a Bernard Shaw play — with carefully prepared, carefully phrased sentences, often with exact and forceful similes, not with the less coherent but more vivid flow of ordinary language, the way people really talk.

Father's Arcane Daughter represents a return to the idea that parents can be selfish and destructive, that children can be harmed when they are not allowed to grow into the people they naturally are. Because the eldest Carmichael child, Caroline, was kidnapped and disappeared apparently without trace years ago, Winston and Hilary are ludicrously over-protected. For Winston this means boredom and being trapped in immaturity; for Hilary the situation is worse, since she suffers from a number of severe handicaps, and her dependence is encouraged by her mother rather than treated as something that she must try to overcome. When a woman appears who claims to be Caroline Carmichael, the prison walls begin to crumble. In many ways this novel makes more explicit the themes that were explored in the earlier books, particularly the full horror of the totally selfish parent, but it seems very low-key; the flashback technique causes a loss of dramatic momentum, and the story itself seems so bizarre that it lacks sufficient credibility. It is unlikely that "Caroline" could carry off her impersonation so successfully; unlikely, too, that the grown-up Hilary, so efficient and brilliant, could really have come from a child so handicapped. And there's something a little too reminiscent of a Bette Davis or a Joan Crawford role in Grace Carmichael; what may be fascinating or horrifying in a great actress on the screen may, in a book, cause only an uncomfortable feeling in the reader that he cannot quite accept as psychologically truthful what he is being told.

Elaine Konigsburg is a novelist of considerable talents, and her most recent books seem to show her trying to exercise her talents in new directions; there is an experimental feeling about these stories that suggests she is searching for some area or theme with which her gifts as a writer can be fully engaged but which, at present, she has not wholly succeeded in finding. When she does, one can expect a book of major interest. Her value to British readers is that she can make something universal out of a setting that is specifically American; in other words, though her writing at its finest may use language and present material and viewpoints that seem thoroughly transatlantic, her children and teenagers could be found in any place; their problems in coming to terms with themselves and with an adult world that at best is messy and at worst corrupt are the problems of the young everywhere.

References

E. L. KONIGSBURG
Jennifer, Hecate, Macbeth, William McKinley, and Me,

> *Elizabeth* Atheneum 1967; Macmillan, London, 1968
> (as *Jennifer, Hecate, Macbeth and Me*)
> *From the Mixed-up Files of Mrs. Basil E. Frankweiler*
> Atheneum 1967; Macmillan, London, 1969
> *About the B'nai Bagels* Atheneum 1969
> *(George)* Atheneum 1970; Macmillan, London 1971
> *Altogether One at a Time* Atheneum 1971
> *A Proud Taste for Scarlet and Miniver* Atheneum 1973;
> Macmillan, London 1974
> *The Dragon in the Ghetto Caper* Atheneum 1974;
> Macmillan, London 1979
> *The Second Mrs. Giaconda* Atheneum 1975;
> Macmillan, London, 1976
> *Father's Arcane Daughter* Atheneum 1976;
> Macmillan, London, 1977

AIDAN CHAMBERS
> "Letter from England" *The Horn Book Magazine,*
> October, 1976

PAUL ZINDEL
> *The Pigman* Harper 1968; Bodley Head 1969

URSULA K. LE GUIN
> *Very Far Away from Anywhere Else* Atheneum 1976;
> Gollancz 1976 (as *A Very Long Way from Anywhere
> Else*)

Viewed From a Squashed Eyeball

♦

PAUL ZINDEL

PAUL ZINDEL is a writer whose novels — especially
The Pigman — are extremely popular on both sides of
the Atlantic; indeed in Britain he is more widely read,
despite the obvious difficulties of his very American
English, than many a British writer whose books teachers
and librarians would prefer that children read.

There is something peculiarly subversive about
Zindel's books that appeals to the adolescent. Adults,
particularly authoritarian figures like policemen or teachers, are usually portrayed in a bad light, and the reader
can feel himself happily encapsulated in an immature
world in which the young are wronged, misunderstood,
and generally knocked about; where the battle-lines between the generations are very clearly drawn; and the
teenager who thinks he's got problems can be at ease,
identify with the central characters, or find he's not the
only misfit, unsuccessful at home or at school, with his
friends, with the opposite sex. Whether life is really like
this is another matter.

For the adult, reading the collected works of Paul
Zindel is a slightly tedious process, which is not the experience one has with some writers of teenage fiction.
The world, in fact, is not as distorted as it appears to be
in these books: it isn't so narrow, so neurotic as this. The
point of view is as out of focus as if someone had quite
literally stepped on the narrator's eyeball. There is also

♦ 25

the problem of narrowness of range in the material; though there are differences in theme and emphasis, Zindel seems essentially to be covering the same ground again and again, and never appears to do it quite so well as he did it in his first novel, *The Pigman*. And there is the famous "style."

Zindel's style is often praised for being the authentic voice of the modern teenager. He "catches the bright, hyperbolic sheen of teenage language accurately and with humor," *The New York Times Book Review* commented, but it seems to me that there is no such thing as "teenage language" any more than there is "adult language." The background and culture of people growing up in Houston, Texas, for example, is going to be so unlike that of people growing up in Boston or London that there are bound to be vast linguistic differences. Zindel's voice, in fact, is specifically that of the New Yorker, and a special kind of New Yorker, too: intellectually very bright and probably of East European origin. It is doubtful whether anybody in real life actually talks like a Zindel character; the hyperboles, the verbal fireworks, the enormous width of vocabulary and cross-reference, though often exceedingly clever and funny, are just too much to accept as everyday speech. His voice is a very useful vehicle for looking at life in the peculiarly lop-sided poses Zindel's characters adopt, but it probably has its origins as much in literature as in reality. As I've said before, it's not so far removed from the voice of Holden Caulfield. The length of Salinger's shadow is extremely odd: Were Holden a real person he would be forty-four today (*The Catcher in the Rye* was published in 1951), doubtless with two or three crazy mixed-up teenage kids of his own. There is, surely, a difference in language between the generations in any age, if only because the world has moved on and become preoccupied with new things. In 1951 the American young were dancing fox-trots and worrying about being drafted for Korea. Holden Caulfield would have known nothing of the drug scene, the beat generation, flower power, sexual permissiveness, Vietnam, pollution, the energy crisis, and a thousand other things that have interested the young since Holden was sixteen. It seems strange, then, to a British adult reader of the same age as Holden would be that today's kids still talk as he does in so many American books.

One only has to open *The Catcher in the Rye* and read the opening sentences to see the similarity to the first paragraph of Zindel's *I Never Loved Your Mind*:

> If you knew I was a seventeen-year-old handsome guy hacking out this verbose volume of literary ecstasy, you'd probably think I was one of those academic genii who run home after a titillating day at school, panting to commence cello lessons. I regret to inform you, however, that I do not suffer from scholasticism of the brain. In fact, I suffer from it so little I dropped out of my puerile, jerky high school exactly eleven months ago.

Even the titles have something in common. "A Perfect Day for Bananafish" or "Just Before the War with the Eskimos" are as joky and esoteric as *My Darling, My Hamburger*, or *Pardon Me, You're Stepping on My Eyeball!*

This kind of writing, if taken in small doses, is witty enough, but read *in extenso* it becomes tiresome. It relies far too much on hyperbole. No car, for instance, ever goes fast in a Zindel novel; it is always burning rubber, or going like a bat out of hell, or traveling at the speed of a Batmobile. People's eyes always widen to the size of balloons or grapefruit. The imagery searches too self-consciously and too often for the exotic, the grotesque, and the ridiculous, so that the reader longs for just one ordinary homely metaphor to leaven the unpalatable richness of the fare. Is Staten Island, for example, really a "sort of geographical version of a detached retina"? Or

♦ 27

would a boy in fact look like "a constipated weasel"? Or someone's hair stick out so much that it "seemed to give him a type of energy like his fingers were jammed into some 220 electric socket"? It's well summed up by the narrator in *Confessions of a Teenage Baboon*:

> I can just walk along a street minding my own business and I'll come across things like a lady sitting on a curb breast-feeding a baby or a man rubbing the back of a hunchbacked girl or some poor guy talking to himself. In other parlance, wherever I go there is the unusual.

It makes the reader doubt the offered realism, the supposed reflection of actualities. Where most of us go, there isn't the unusual.

Most irritating of all is the repetitiveness. John's mother in *The Pigman* "runs around like a chicken with its head cut off," but so do Jacqueline *and* Miss Conlin in *Pardon Me, You're Stepping on My Eyeball!* In the latter book there are "wall-to-wall crooks," and in *The Undertaker's Gone Bananas* "wall-to-wall teenagers," though Mae West did that one first with "wall-to-wall men," long before the Second World War. When somebody is disliked, he's always "retarded" or has "a low IQ" (even a peacock in *The Pigman* has a low IQ) or he's "Neanderthal" or "Cro-magnon man" or has a memory "like that of a titmouse with curvature of the brain." Amusing once, yes; half a dozen times, no. One passage in *The Pigman* repeats the same phrase six times when once would be enough:

> And there was her sick mother — very thin and with this smile frozen on her face — right in the middle of the living room! That was the strange part. Miss Stewart kept her mother in this bed right in the middle of the living room, and it almost made me cry. She made a little joke about it — how she kept her mother in the middle of the living room because she didn't want her to think she was missing anything when people came to visit. Can you imagine keeping your sick

mother in a bed right smack in the middle of the living room? When I look at Miss Reillen I feel sorry. When I hear her walking I feel even more sorry for her because maybe she keeps her mother in a bed in the middle of the living room much like Miss Stewart. Who would want to marry a woman that keeps her sick mother in a bed right in the middle of the living room?

Incidents and characters are too often repeated in the books. There are teenage parties that get out of hand – brilliantly done in *The Pigman* and *I Never Loved Your Mind;* absurdly over-exaggerated and unconvincing in *Pardon Me, You're Stepping on My Eyeball!* and *Confessions of a Teenage Baboon.* There are car chases; alcoholics; boys searching for father-figures – a theme better handled by Paula Fox in *Blowfish Live in the Sea.* Rather oddly, Zindel has a penchant for characters whose professions are connected with medicine: Dewey and Yvette in *I Never Loved Your Mind* are hospital orderlies, and so is Rod Gittens in *My Darling, My Hamburger;* Lorraine's mother in *The Pigman* is a peripatetic nurse who is also a kleptomaniac; and so is Chris's mother in *Confessions of a Teenage Baboon.* One such oddity of this nature is surely enough: two strain credulity. The baboon imagery also occurs in *The Pigman;* funeral parlors are used in both *The Pigman* and *The Undertaker's Gone Bananas.*

In all his books there is the occasional schmaltz protruding through the hard brittle surface, which shows, underneath the bright jazzy exterior of the language, a curiously mushy center: at the graduation ceremony, for instance, in *My Darling, My Hamburger,* "The slow sounding of the drum pervaded everywhere like the heartbeat of a giant, and the lines began to move, slowly, solemnly." The final sentence of *Pardon Me, You're Stepping on My Eyeball!* – "In an instant there was the explosion of the last stage of the rocket, and then, at last, there were the stars set in their proper place" – is echoed, in an even more glossy romantic wording at the end of *Confessions of a Teenage Baboon*:

> I reached out and took Rosemary's hand in mine and we sat there a long, long time. Then, after a while, I began to look past the moon, past all the great satellites of Jupiter, and dream upon the stars.

Such fuzzy sentimentality is perhaps the inescapable partner of the bitter glittering cynicism that is the usual tone; both together add up to the voice of immaturity.

It may seem odd to complain of immaturity in novels for teenagers, especially when the author's voice is not necessarily that of his creations — difficult though that may be to suggest in a first-person narrative. One suspects that the mouthpiece in all Zindel's books is not really the character — John Conlan or Dewey Daniels — but Paul Zindel: and that may well be the reason why reading him is, in some ways, a disappointing experience for the adult. People who write novels for children and teenagers may well be using the creative process as a way of rearranging the patterns of their childhood or adolescence, as an exorcism of their hang-ups — indeed we are, all of us, probably doing that — but the art of it is to disguise it so well that it doesn't show through. There is something so frenetic and hysterical about some of Zindel's work that one suspects personal experiences which may underlie some of the material in the books are still uncomfortable and too emotionally close for him to become sufficiently detached to give them a separate life of their own in a novel.

The Pigman, his first book, is probably his best. It is a somber and chastening story that gets better and better as it goes on, and despite the linguistic irritations, it deserves its high reputation and wide readership. More than any other of his novels it has coherent shape and direction, and its climax is particularly good: a chilling, sobering, morality-tale conclusion. It also has several finely-wrought verbal felicities: "It's sort of spooky how when you're caught talking to God nowadays everybody thinks you're nuts. They used to call you a prophet" is one example. Lorraine and John are credible realistic characters, telling us more, strangely, about each other in their first-person narrations than about themselves. Effective, too, is the emphasis laid by the author on the fact that it is a combination of their own selfishness and Mr. Pignati's that leads to the old man's death — not some vague malevolent adult world outside that is responsible, which is the point made in some of the other books. Mr. Pignati's premature senility and the dangerously unstable state of his mind are quite unrecognized by the children and provide the necessary recipe for disaster; one watches the collision of these two utterly different life-styles — the Pigman's and the children's — knowing all along that, whatever the pleasures each may give to the other, tragedy is bound to be the outcome, because none of the protagonists can ever see beyond what is happening at the present moment. It is a fine book, but one can't help feeling that a completely different change of direction might have been best for Zindel in his second novel.

The characters in *My Darling, My Hamburger* are less sharply individualized; in fact they seem little more than four standard teenage types — blond attractive girl with lots of poise, mousy introverted girl with no poise, rich and handsome boy, plain and not so well-to-do boy. The main theme of the book — Liz's abortion — is dealt with fairly well; the whole business comes over, as it should, as an ugly, emotionally messy, squalid experience. But the dice are far too heavily loaded against Liz. Quirks of fate play a large role in what happens, and her encounters with the unbelievably nasty Rod Gittens seem a little too much when added to the chain of circumstantial events that leads to her and Sean Collins making love ♦ 31 without any contraceptive precautions. Also the book seems, ten years later, rather unmodern. The horror of the back-street abortion, even if still with us, is not now necessarily the outcome of an unwanted pregnancy, and the whole atmosphere of the teenage romance as portrayed here has a passé feeling to it with its formal dates and dances. It's as if the author felt as unrelaxed as his characters. Maybe the trouble is that the book is too didactic, and that not enough space is devoted to developing what goes on inside the characters: one feels curiously uninvolved with them, unlike, say, in *The Pigman*.

Or in *I Never Loved Your Mind*. The verbal pyrotechnics of this novel are more mannered and excessive than in most of the others, and some of the situations — the nude vacuum-cleaning scene, for instance — are somewhat unreal, yet Dewey Daniels is a complex, sympathetic character who holds our attention throughout. He is far from "heartless," as the *Times Literary Supplement* reviewer called him. It is impressive that Zindel is honest enough to admit that Dewey's chase of Yvette is not because he loves her, but simply because he wants to go to bed with her (a common enough teenage situation, surely, but one not frequently acknowledged as being normal and healthy in teenage fiction). Indeed, who could love such a monster of selfish egotism as Yvette? One is less convinced when, having slept with her, he does fall in love with the creature, neatly ironic though that may be. Yvette's world of unrecognized double standards, hypocrisy and parasitism — Zindel's comment on the worst excesses of flower power and the whole late-sixties dropout scene — is done with a great deal of panache and excellent satirical humor, and though the details of that particular era are a phenomenon of the recent past rather than the present, they don't have the dated feeling of his treatment of the Senior Prom stuff of *My Darling, My Hamburger*. They are brought to life much more persuasively. The ending is good, too; Dewey's decision to abandon "that Love Land crap" in order to do something "phantasmagorically different" yet not "to give civilization a kick in the behind" is not a suggestion that he's going to join the nine-to-five rat-race, but rather that he will follow a path of self-fulfilment, whatever that may turn out to be. The *Times Literary Supplement* is again wrong in saying that he decides to train as a doctor; maybe he will, but Dewey's remark about pursuing a medical career is probably no more than a handy excuse to give his resignation from his job some plausibility. It's an effective and satisfying conclusion.

Pardon Me, You're Stepping on My Eyeball! and *Confessions of a Teenage Baboon* are Zindel's least impressive books. It's difficult, in fact, to say anything good about either of them. The plots are improbable, the tone unrelievedly hysterical, and most of the characters so grotesque that it's almost impossible to suspend disbelief at any point. The few ordinary kids — Edna in *Pardon Me, You're Stepping on My Eyeball!* and Chris and Rosemary in *Confessions of a Teenage Baboon* — seem so out of place in this world of nightmare that one wonders what they're doing there at all, let alone being allowed to grow up and come to terms with their problems. It's more likely that they'd collapse and be carted off to a lunatic asylum. It's not easy to believe that someone as normal, as nice and sensible as Edna is, would be in the care of a school psychiatrist, labeled as one of the most maladjusted of children, unless the whole world has gone completely mad. It's equally difficult to accept the idea that Chris would be so attracted, so spell-bound by the neurotic, dangerous, suicidal Lloyd, no matter what flashes of common sense and insight a thirty-year-old who's never grown up may have. This is a pity, because the man who has failed to mature, who still wants as an adult to be King of the Teenagers, is an interesting idea. But Zindel fails to breathe real life into Lloyd. He's too ◆ 33 bizarre, far too strange to have the attraction to the young that Zindel says he has. Such a figure *is* dangerous, just as the senile Mr. Pignati is dangerous, but the disaster that occurs would be much more effective if the reader could be allowed to feel sympathy for Lloyd similar to that which he feels for the Pigman. It's as if Zindel had approached his material too emotively and had not properly sized up all the delicate nuances of a complex situation. The characters in these books indulge in too much self-pity; there is too much straining after big emotional effects: the reader is left unconvinced and, again, uninvolved.

The Undertaker's Gone Bananas shows some signs of the new direction which Zindel should perhaps have pursued after *The Pigman*, or at the very latest after *I Never Loved Your Mind*. The world of this novel is a younger world, though the central characters, we are told, are fifteen. But despite Bobby's ability to drive a car, and other small details which suggest that particular age, he and Lauri give the feeling, emotionally and psychologically, of being younger — thirteen-year-olds perhaps. The mechanics of the plot, too, belong to a species of children's fiction — kids outwit police in catching crooks — that is the property of readers younger than those who would enjoy *I Never Loved Your Mind*. In fact the story is very well handled: Bobby seeing the next door neighbor, Mr. Hulka, murdering his wife, and the police refusing to believe him, may sound a bit old hat as a plot but it's told with skill, humor, and real excitement, proving in fact to be an excellent addition to what one might think was an overworked genre. Bobby's precociousness and daring is nicely balanced by Lauri's caution and good sense, and for once the adults — the Hulkas excepted — are not seen as totally unsympathetic monsters, but normal credible people. Even the grumbles and threats of the police are the reactions of uncorrupt ordinary men trying to do a difficult job. It's as if Zindel has at last worked something out of his system, and is now able to look at his creations in a more objective light, and, as a result, do something that is much more satisfactory than the two previous books.

The Undertaker's Gone Bananas is a welcome development. Zindel had clearly more than exhausted, with *Confessions of a Teenage Baboon*, a very narrow and limited kind of material. *The Undertaker's Gone Bananas* certainly shows greater control than *Confessions of a Teenage Baboon* — the language is more restrained, the climaxes are not spoiled by being too frenetic, the view of things is no longer that of a squashed eyeball. The world is here a richer, more varied place than it seemed previously.

References

PAUL ZINDEL
>   *The Pigman* Harper 1968; Bodley Head 1969
>   *My Darling, My Hamburger* Harper 1969; Bodley Head 1970
>   *I Never Loved Your Mind* Harper 1970; Bodley Head 1971
>   *Pardon Me, You're Stepping on My Eyeball!* Harper 1976; Bodley Head 1976
>   *Confessions of a Teenage Baboon* Harper 1977; Bodley Head 1978
>   *The Undertaker's Gone Bananas* Harper 1978; Bodley Head 1979

J. D. SALINGER
>   *The Catcher in the Rye* Little 1951; Hamish Hamilton 1951
>   "A Perfect Day for Bananafish"; "Just Before the War with the Eskimos" from *Nine Stories* Little 1953; Hamish Hamilton 1953 (as *For Esmé with Love and Squalor*)

PAULA FOX
>   *Blowfish Live in the Sea* Bradbury 1970; Macmillan, London, 1972

Achieving One's
Heart's Desires

◆

PHILIPPA PEARCE

In England Philippa Pearce is regarded by almost everyone who has any connection at all with the world of children's books as the outstanding author of our time and in America, where she is also widely read and highly respected, she is considered a writer of the greatest importance. *Tom's Midnight Garden,* her masterpiece, is the yardstick with which we tend to measure everything else, and we usually find that everything else does not quite reach it in quality, even if we are forced to admit that in places it does fall short of perfection. It seems to me that on the whole Philippa Pearce deserves her reputation, but we are probably wrong to think of *Tom's Midnight Garden* as simply the best children's novel of the twentieth century. The issue is more complicated than that. It is the best of a certain kind of children's book: the sensitive fantasy set in a timeless English landscape; the gentle, brooding rural story in which British writers excel. But to compare it with a realistic novel that has a harsh urban background — Robert Westall's *The Machine Gunners,* for example — is not altogether possible. Different criteria are involved.

One of the most remarkable things about Philippa Pearce is the smallness of her output: only four novels in nearly a quarter of a century of writing. There have, it is true, been several volumes of short stories, and in 1978, *The Battle of Bubble and Squeak,* a book that is in length about half-way between a short story and a novel. It is a great disappointment that she hasn't written more, but whatever the reasons for this may be, it is a fact that her admirers have to accept. Maybe she has said all she has to say, and has wisely decided not to write just for the sake of pleasing other people. Some of the short stories are superb; "The Tree in the Meadow," for instance, is an object lesson in how to master the genre. But it is the novels on which her reputation rests, and the first of these was *Minnow on the Say*.

Minnow on the Say employs a familiar formula for a children's book — the successful search for a long-buried treasure, with its usual attendant props: the false clues, villain racing to beat the children in their quest, etc. If the book were no more than this it would scarcely be worth writing about, but it is unusual in many respects; and it is worth noting that none of the subsequent novels employs such a well-tried device. The main characters — Adam, David, and Miss Codling — are drawn with a convincing detail that immediately places the book on a higher level than its plot suggests. Adam has many of the characteristics of the heroes of *Tom's Midnight Garden* and *A Dog So Small*, particularly their passionate obsession to achieve their hearts' desires. Adam is irrational, often bad-tempered, often depressed; he swings mercurially from one extreme emotion to another. So Miss Codling's string is thrown away in anger; the rare Empress of China rose is destroyed. At other times he gives up in despair, retires to his bed, or digs up the dogs' graves (to David's horror) in his search. He shares Miss Codling's love for the very bricks and mortar of the house they live in; if Codlings is sold, then Adam feels something of himself will be destroyed with it. He is much the most interesting character in the book, and altogether a surprising person to find in a quiet and leisurely English children's novel.

David, in contrast, is practical and down-to-earth, much the sort of son we would expect of Bob Moss, who drives the country buses and grows prize roses. Yet Bob Moss was once known as Bad Bobby Moss, Terror of both the Barleys; and David too, experiences the longing, the unfulfilled desire that torments all Philippa Pearce's heroes:

> Waiting a long time, with a full-sized boat bobbing at your own landing stage – it was very hard. David thought he could never bear it.

Also, like Tom Long in his garden, or Ben Blewitt swimming with the dog Tilly in the River Say, he delights in the sensuousness of the summer countryside:

> David was stirred by so deep an excitement that he stood as in a trance of feeling; he felt the warmth of the sun on his neck; he heard the soft humming of the bees; he smelt the leaves of the apple-mint that had strayed over the neglected path and been trodden and crushed underfoot.

Mr. Smith, too, has an obsession about finding the treasure, but he is one of the book's failures. He is observed at such a distance and so unsympathetically as to be scarcely credible. The author is not really interested; Mr. Smith is no more than a necessary piece of the plot – the one scene in his house, curtains drawn and weak disembodied voice, is unnecessarily melodramatic, and his relationship with his daughter, Elizabeth, is like that of Mr. Rochester and his wife in *Jane Eyre*, and no more convincing. Elizabeth never succeeds in being credible either; and the recognition scene between her and Adam is particularly weak. Melodrama in fact is the book's main defect; in the last part of the story in particular one larger-than-life scene succeeds another. There is the death of old Mr. Codling (another improbable character), the last-minute race to catch the bus, David's confrontation with Mr. Smith at the bus station, David's resolve (out of character) to sink the canoe, and Elizabeth showering David with orchids from a passing train. There is a deterioration in quality. Here the pace slackens, too many interviews take place behind closed doors and have to be reported, the denouement is slow and an anti-climax. But it must be said that all the succeeding books are totally free of these particular faults.

Minnow on the Say seems to go wrong at the point where the Smiths enter the story, and perhaps the deterioration is because the author clearly dislikes Mr. Smith, "not perhaps the nicest kind of business man — he is certainly one of the most selfish and stupid." Philippa Pearce's least successful creations seem to be people she dislikes — Mrs. Melbourne, Sir Robert Hatton — though these are not as unconvincing as Mr. Smith.

Squeak Wilson's fear of everyone, particularly of Adam, is, however, a very amusing piece of caricature: in fact, the behavior of everybody in the book is seen at one time or another with an amused or ironic eye. There is Miss Codling's extravagant folly, and David's comment to her: "Will you be having footmen and things?" The children speculate wildly at one stage about whether it would be possible to drug Miss Codling and there is Adam's conviction that "Smith is only a name people assume to escape the police." After a long pause David says, "Smith is sometimes a real name," but Adam persuades him that this is not so, and David's "head whirled with wild new doubts."

For all its faults, *Minnow on the Say* is an impressive first novel. It could never be mistaken for a book by anybody else, despite its well-worn storyline, for the virtues that delight us in the succeeding books are already there. Ultimately it is not the treasure-hunt or the Smiths that we remember so much as Miss Codling's anxieties and dignity, the unusualness of Adam, the quiet pastoral background of the Barleys, the boys' and the author's sensuous delight in the river — absent from hardly any page ◆ 39 of the book — and the warmth and naturalness of David's home and family. The voice we associate with the later books is already there — the rendering of the sensuous physical world, linking it so often with a past that is only just under the surface, in sentences in which rhythms and cadences express exactly the right pleasure or sadness that the words mean.

Tom's Midnight Garden is, as I have said, not without its faults, and striking though the imaginative conception of the story is, I am not sure that from the point of view of craftsmanship the two subsequent novels are not better done. The opening chapters seem laboriously written, the characters a little wooden, and measles is certainly not a good enough reason for packing Tom off to his Aunt Gwen's. However when Tom enters the garden, all is well; the writing loses its uncertainty and seems to change into a triumphantly major key; it is as if the author, having eventually got her central character into the situation she is most interested in, is relieved at being able, at last, to say what she wants to say:

> There is a time, between night and day, when landscapes sleep. Only the earliest riser sees that hour; or the all-night traveller, letting up the blind of his railway-carriage window, will look out on a rushing landscape of stillness, in which trees and bushes and plants stand immobile and breathless in sleep — wrapped in sleep, as the traveller himself wrapped his body in his great-coat or his rug the night before.

Like Adam Codling, Tom Long is obsessed by one fixed idea. This is to explain to himself the mystery of the garden, and ultimately to stay in it forever. Other children in the book, Tom's brother Peter and Hatty Melbourne, are as single-minded and passionately concerned with their own longings as Tom is: Peter with joining Tom in the garden (some of the most moving writing in the book expresses Peter's frustration at being left out of things), and Hatty with finding her own satisfactory *modus vivendi* in the unsympathetic Melbourne family. Hatty grows up into a spirited and independent woman and as she does so her longings and frustrations seem to fall away. Circumstances are certainly on her side rather than on her aunt's but her happiness as an adult seems to reinforce a feeling that pervades the whole book: that children of Tom's age experience joy and disappointment with an intensity that adults hardly ever realize. It is the force with which this intensity is expressed that is one of the book's main strengths:

> "I do then!" said Peter, "I do! I lie awake at night and wish I were there; then I fall asleep and dream that I am there. I want to go — I do — I do!"
> "But why, Peter, why?" asked his mother. Peter only cast his eyes down and repeated in a flat obstinate voice that he knew that he would like it.

Most moving of all perhaps, in its intensity, is Tom's final attempt to get back into the garden he has lost forever; he crashes into a fence and dustbins; runs "like a rat with the dogs after it"; his screams wake the whole house; he "sobbed and fought as though he were being taken prisoner"; and as he wakes the next day, "even as his mind stirred awake, the horror and grief of yesterday were already there. This was Saturday; he had lost his chance; he had lost the garden. Today he went home."

As well as this intensity, the characters share other characteristics: impulsiveness, unreasonableness, even rudeness, adults as well as children. Mrs. Melbourne is utterly unreasonable in her attitude towards Hatty; she even despises her son James for taking pity on the girl. Aunt Gwen is as impulsive as Hatty:

> "I wish I hadn't to go home tomorrow," said Tom. He dared not go farther, but he spoke loudly. Aunt Gwen gave a cry of amazement and delight, and actually clapped her hands. "Would you like to stay?"
> "Yes."
> "Several days more? Another week?"
> "Or more," said Tom.

"We'll send a telegram at once," said Aunt Gwen, and ran out.

In contrast with this feverishness of emotion in almost all the characters the landscape has a cool, unchanging certainty about it; this was the function of landscape, particularly the river, in *Minnow on the Say* and Tom's garden, though its seasons may alter, or lightning on one occasion strike down a tree, is always there, inviting, full of promise:

> Every night he was able to steal downstairs as usual, into the garden; and there the feverishness of his chill always left him, as though the very greenness of trees and plants and grass cooled his blood.

The "magic" of the garden is that it is a Garden of Eden, a symbol of Tom's and Hatty's innocence; they have to leave it as they grow up — Tom's appearances become rarer as Hatty grows older and he grows to think that she can see through him. It is no coincidence that when Tom finds himself excluded finally it is Hatty's wedding day. Hatty is in love with Barty, so she has no more need of her imaginary friend; Tom is banished simply because she doesn't think of him any more. The relationship between Tom and Hatty is like an innocent love affair in this Garden of Eden; and other parallels with the Book of Genesis can be seen — Adam and his descendants were gardeners, according to tradition; Adam's sons were Cain and Abel; Mrs. Melbourne's gardener is called Abel. But in his simplicity and religious devotion, he is inside Eden with Tom and Hatty, not outside like the Abel of Genesis. However, just as Eden was destroyed so is this garden; sold off by James for building land. One other parallel with Eden is Tom's dream:

> He went downstairs to go into the garden; but he found that the angel had come down from the clock-face and — grown to giant-size — barred the way with a flaming sword.

If the garden is Eden, then, it means that the past, and particularly the late Victorian period, is seen as a golden age. Hatty says of the river: "The boys bathe in it only a little farther downstream where there are pools; and they fish." Later, when Aunt Gwen takes Tom for a walk, they meet a man fishing:

> "There aren't any fish," the man replied sourly. He stood by a notice that said: "WARNING. The Council takes no responsibility for persons bathing, wading or paddling. These waters have been certified as unsuitable for such purposes, owing to pollution."

And Tom notices that "there was a large quantity of broken glass, broken crockery and empty tins dimly to be seen on the river-bed." Aunt Gwen and Uncle Alan are obviously preferable as people to Mrs. Melbourne, but there is something mean and circumscribed about their way of life in a flat compared with the grandeur of the Melbournes' house. Tom finds them insufferably dull. Incidentally, one of the minor successes of the book seems to me to be Uncle Alan; his irascibility and total lack of understanding of his sensitive imaginative nephew are very convincingly done.

Many people reading the book for the first time, who have not noticed that Mrs. Bartholomew and Hatty are one and the same person, speak of the almost unbearable tension as the book proceeds into what looks like an inescapable tragedy, their sense of relief when this is averted, and their delight that the ending is so credible. The fact that the ending is not just a happy coda stuck on so that the reader won't be upset, is because Hatty *is* Mrs. Bartholomew, and always was, since before the beginning of the book. In other words, the author knows precisely what she is about. The clues are all there for us, early on. The first appearance of Mrs. Bartholomew is when she comes downstairs to wind up • 43 the clock, a sort of Father Time figure. A page is spent on showing this seemingly irrelevant character carrying out a seemingly insignificant action, but as the clock is the great link between time past and time present, and Mrs. Bartholomew is shown as its keeper or guardian now (just as the angel on the dial is its keeper in time past), it seems clear that the purpose of the scene is to suggest that she has a much more important connection with the past than Tom, at the moment, realizes. And at the end of the chapter, when Tom enters the garden for the first time, the game is virtually given away by a further apparently irrelevant comment. Mrs. Bartholomew

> was lying tranquilly in bed; her false teeth, in a glass of water by the bedside, grinned unpleasantly in the moonlight, but her indrawn mouth was curved in a smile of easy sweet-dreaming sleep. She was dreaming of the scenes of her childhood.

And if the penny still hasn't dropped, we should be wondering not long after why one of the Melbournes' friends is called Barty.

Another reason why the ending seems so effective is because the author herself seems to be growing up as a novelist in the process of writing this book. There is a great difference in the quality of the last chapters compared with the first; not only is there simply more certainty and maturity in the way the language of the sentences is put together with their increasing poetry, subtlety of rhythm and cadence, but the insights and sympathies deepen all the time; we feel that the author has a more profound knowledge of Tom and Hatty at the end than she had at the beginning. The same is true of Tom's relationship with the Kitsons; it is developing all the time in sympathy, and in humor. Nevertheless it must be said that the problems of that relationship remains unsolved. Alan and Gwen are no nearer understanding Tom than they were at the beginning, and the debt of gratitude Tom should owe them is scarcely commented on. The speculation about the nature of time grows more thoughtful as the book continues; Tom's ideas on the subject become more complex and adult, and his imaginative leaps seem to hold more truth than Uncle Alan's scientific explanations.

Probably the most impressive writing in the book is the chapter called "Skating," not only for its superb evocation of the frostbound Cambridgeshire countryside, but for its description of the interior of Ely Cathedral and the tomb of the man who "exchanged time for eternity." There is a vivid pictorial rendering of what the eye really sees: "They skated on, and the thin, brilliant sun was beginning to set, and Hatty's black shadow flitted along at their right hand, across the dazzle of the ice." Or what the ear really hears — "the ice hissed with their passage." The certainty with which these things are done not only shows a great advance on *Minnow on the Say*, but a complete mastery of language that is unrivalled among living writers of children's books. Only Paula Fox comes near this kind of quality.

I can think of only one blemish in her next book, *A Dog So Small*, and that is the somewhat irrelevant story of what happened to the picture after Ben lost it, which seems to show the old unfortunate taste for melodrama. But in Ben Blewitt we have the most interesting of Philippa Pearce's heroes. Though she tells us more than once that Ben is a perfectly ordinary boy, we can scarcely believe her; Ben is surely the oddest person she has ever written about. No other character in her novels departs so far from reality into his private obsession as Ben does; Tom Long's fantasy world was confined to night time but Ben's operates during the day as well as in his dreams, and this leads to real disaster — "a broken leg, three broken ribs, a broken collarbone and concussion." Ben's problems with his family do not come solely from the fact that he is the odd one out in age; he is also the only one with any real sensitivity or imagination. This is well illustrated in the first chapter by the remarks on Russia:

> His father read about Russia in the newspaper, and thumped on the table. Paul and Frankie read about Russian space-travel.

But for Ben, Russia

> was always under deep dazzling snow. The land was a level and endless white, with here and there a dark forest, where wolves crouched in the day-time, to come out at night, howling and ravening.

Ben has an additional problem that none of the heroes of the other novels has to face; there is no possible outlet for his frustration, no person sufficiently unpleasant for him to dislike or blame. *A Dog So Small* has no villain. The Blewitt family are remarkable for their niceness, so Ben's troubles turn in on himself, leading him into difficulties at school, quarrels with his parents and brothers, his frequently repeated desire just to be left alone, and eventually the accident. This withdrawal from reality, the author suggests, is sad and reprehensible. Ben causes his family considerable unhappiness as well as a ruined Christmas, and Mrs. Blewitt's wish to know what is wrong with her son is never satisfied. The car driver who knocked him down is unnerved and upset for a considerable time; Ben even makes such a casual contact as the librarian feel uneasy. The answer is that the Blewitt parents should have given Ben a dog in the first place; had they known what damage the absence of a dog was causing him they would almost certainly have done so. But they never know, and this points to another sadness in this book — that even in the nicest of families real communication between its members can be impossible.

The construction of *A Dog So Small* is interesting; its opening pages and its conclusion contain the most memorable passages. Like *Tom's Midnight Garden* it opens with the hero's world crashing about his ears; Ben's dis-

covery that he has not been given a dog for his birthday
would be so easy to sentimentalize, but in fact the author
is quite merciless, showing no let-up in the portrayal of
Ben's disappointment, every humorous and uncomprehending remark from his family making the situation worse
and worse. Ben is not allowed any escape from the moral
dilemma; it would be so easy if he could just quietly hate
his grandparents but Grandpa Fitch has written "TRULY
SORY ABOUT DOG" and for Ben there is no way out
of that. So Ben's feelings, here as elsewhere, turn in-
wards. The last chapter, too, could so easily be a sentimental happy ending. Instead we have something that is
psychologically far more truthful; as Granny Fitch says,
"People get their heart's desire, and then they have to
learn how to live with it." Ben makes the miserable discovery that a real dog, given to him at last, is no adequate
substitute for the chihuahua of his imagination. It would
be a cruelly tragic ending if Ben were to leave Brown on
the Heath in the growing dusk; right up to the last page
it looks as if he will. But he does not, fortunately. By
this I don't mean I necessarily want the book to end
happily (it would be interesting to know if the author at
any time intended to allow Ben to abandon the dog; certainly a publisher might be shy of such an ending) but
the reasons and feelings Ben has for keeping the dog are
consistent with the development of his character in the
last third of the book. Since the accident he has begun
to grow up, to accept, however slowly, the fact that he
has to live in the real world — "He saw that if you didn't
have the possible things, then you had nothing." This
book, more than the others, charts the changes and growth
of a child's personality. The effect of not being given a
dog is delayed by the visit to his grandparents (Tilly is
some sort of compensation); the full weight of despair
sets in on his return to London — he won't make any
Christmas presents, join in the preparations for his sister's
wedding — but sinks into a morose solitude. Then there is

the accident, after which he reappraises the previous events in a more adult way, and eventually returns to normality.

The use of caricature is widespread; a number of people and events are seen almost entirely in terms of amused, wry exaggeration. Our first views of Mrs. Fitch — coming backwards downstairs — and Mr. Fitch tied up in his own dog's lead are Dickensian, and this impression is reinforced when we think of the Blewitt family in comparison with the Cratchits, particularly in the scene of the Christmas preparations; there is the storm when Ben reads the Bible to his grandmother, and her interpolations, "that Jehovah . . . could have done with a bit more Christian charity sometimes!" and Grandpa Fitch in the hospital, frightened at everything, "nearly knocking his chair over, and treading on his hat," turning to that hat for succor: he "looked intently inside it, but seemed not to find there any suggestion of what he should say." It is caricature of the best sort in that our belief in the reality of these people is never in doubt; the author has as much sympathy for them as amusement. One is reminded of Dickens in a quite different way by the description of the fog, and as in *Bleak House*, fog in the country is contrasted with fog in the city. The language used however is not at all like that used by Dickens: "And the soft whiteness of the fog drifted up to the window, pressed against the glass and looked in on them."

A boy longing for a dog: it is a common theme in children's fiction. The unusualness of *A Dog So Small* lies in its ability to suggest the sheer pleasure humans can derive from the animal world, and the intensity some people feel for animals when there is an emotional gap left by the deficiencies of human beings. The dogs in this novel never cease to be dogs. Philippa Pearce never falls into the obvious cliché of endowing them with human or superhuman feelings. It is an obvious pitfall and one that Enid Blyton, for example, falls into in *Five Go Off in a Caravan*:

> In two minutes they were all asleep on the grass except Timmy. If his family fell asleep like this, Timmy considered himself on guard. The big dog gave his mistress George a soft lick and sat up firmly beside her, his ears cocked, and his eyes bright.

The tired style of this passage comes as much from the cliché of making the dog think as a human might as from any other fault. Tilly's pups are *really* there: "he shifted the puppy into one hand — which it slightly overflowed"; another pup barks for the first time in its life, and looks round to see where the sound comes from; together they are "a large, thick, sleek blob of multiple puppy-life."

The Children of the House was a story originally written for adults by Brian Fairfax-Lucy, but Philippa Pearce rewrote it as a children's book. Stylistically, it is entirely hers. It has four main characters, unlike the single hero of the two preceding novels, or the pair of *Minnow on the Say*. And though this is the saddest of all the books, there is nevertheless an emphasis on the companionship and pleasures of friendship between the brothers and sisters, in direct contrast with the family in *A Dog So Small* which splits into a pair of brothers, Paul and Frankie, and a pair of sisters, May and Dilys, leaving Ben, number three of five, a solitary. Paula Fox, in *The Stone-Faced Boy*, also emphasizes the loneliness of the third child in a family of five. Margaret in *The Children of the House* we are told "wished above all for the companionship of the other three"— the very thing that ultimately is denied her; she only wishes to exist as a member of a group, an adjunct of the others, and this over-riding desire fills her with a singular horror when Hugh and Laura quarrel, and gives the writing a poignancy and total sense of loss when she is separated from them, a feeling of existence having no further meaning:

> All was quiet; but there was nothing to do, nobody to talk to. She watched out of the window until outside grew dark. Then she turned up the lamp and waited,

> with the door open, for her supper. As she sat, the schoolroom seemed to get larger and the passage outside wider and longer, like a dark street in a town. Then the between-maid came with her supper of soup and a cake. "And Alice says, go to bed when you have finished, and she will be up later."

However, much of the book concerns the adventures the children share together, the raid on the kitchen garden, the discovery of the half crown, the search for moorhens' eggs. The others grow up, Tom and Laura are impatient to leave, only Margaret wants to play "Do you remember?" Laura cannot leave quickly enough; we are told more than once that she is a girl of spirit, that she has her father's high temper and determination. Tom also wants to leave, to be a soldier; he is pathetically unaware of what we, with the hindsight of history, know is waiting for him. This Tom is a very different boy from his namesake in *Tom's Midnight Garden*. He is adventurous, a natural leader, even reckless; he never thinks of the consequences of his actions, and often lands the other children and the servants in trouble. He is particularly thoughtless in the episode involving Margaret's descent in the well, and quite insensitive to her fright. He is, surprisingly, a coward:

> Tom was very pale. He knew the other three were watching him, waiting for him to speak. In the past they had always relied upon him, but often — although they would never admit it — he had let them down. Laura was remembering those occasions as she watched him: he could see it in her eyes.

A minor theme of the book is Tom's cowardice and his successful attempt to overcome it; his standing up to his parents and daring to point out their faults, not in the heat of the moment, but with calculated forethought, is his first step on the road to his posthumous Victoria Cross.

50 •

Hugh is more in the tradition of Philippa Pearce's previous heroes — Adam, Tom Long, Ben. He has the same passion (an example is his furious disgust with Tom, when Tom wonders whether the stone breaker deserves to be given a shilling) and shrinks from situations of possible violence that his brother might relish:

> In thick black type: WAR DECLARED. Hugh saw it, and felt himself go cold, breathless, dizzy. He sat down in a chair. He felt that the end of the world had come.

Like Margaret, he cannot bear separation from the others. The train journey to boarding school is the first time he had "ever shut the nursery door behind him with such finality upon the rocking-horse, the white cat, the green parrot, the portrait of W. G. Grace" and his "eyelids and eyes were tired already with private tears." Even if we say that this is what our own reactions would be, it is worth pointing out that they certainly wouldn't be Laura's and probably not Tom's.

This sharp distinction of character is necessary in a book in which four people are sharing the same activities. It is worth noting that *The Children of the House* is the only novel by Philippa Pearce in which girls play a central role, in which we look at the world through the eyes of the girls as well as the boys. There is, of course, Hatty in *Tom's Midnight Garden*, but we rarely observe Tom from her point of view; it is usually the other way round. Less successful creations in *The Children of the House* are the parents, Sir Robert and Lady Hatton, particularly Sir Robert. The author is trying to emphasize in this novel that life fifty or sixty years ago is not the pleasant magic world lost beyond recall of *Tom's Midnight Garden*. One aspect of life that was less satisfactory was the relationship between parents and children, but Sir Robert Hatton does not come off as a credible Victorian-Edwardian father, conscious of status, chilling and distant to his children; he seems inhumane, improbable, devoid of any parental feelings at all:

> Sir Robert had favourite topics on which he liked to lecture them. He lectured all four on the continuous and crippling cost of their upkeep. Separately, he lectured Tom on the expense of his education and his lack of gratitude; Hugh on his idleness, which would end in his breaking stones on the road for a living; Laura on the unlikelihood of her making a good marriage. To Margaret he said nothing: his ignoring of her might have been the worst of all, except that Margaret was always glad to escape notice of any sort.

Lady Hatton, it is stressed, is of a kinder disposition than her husband; she has the good of the children at heart, though she makes the great mistake of putting the upkeep of the house before the children's needs. Her concern is for Stanford, and her desire to preserve unchanged a way of life that is already anachronistic. Yet she makes an attempt to understand her children's behavior.

> Their mother had not joined in the storming. Walter reported that she was sorry for it all; thought the children had not meant any harm; considered that they had been punished enough by the dreadful realization that Margaret might well have been drowned; and pointed out that they had otherwise begun the holidays with perfect behavior.

Nevertheless the effect of this is largely cancelled out by the author showing us, in one of the few scenes in which we actually see Lady Hatton with her children, that she can be as frightening and bad-tempered as Sir Robert — the episode in which the children object to the clothes they are supposed to wear at the dinner party.

It seems as if *The Children of the House* was written as a deliberate corrective to the view of the past suggested in *Tom's Midnight Garden*. Though Mrs. Melbourne is as nasty as Sir Robert Hatton, she has, ultimately, little effect on her niece; and we are constantly aware of the beauty and variety of the garden in the past compared with the sordid present in which the garden is split up into little plots; villas have been built; dustbins, garages and tarmac have replaced lawns and hyacinth beds. In *The Children of the House*, Stanford is a white elephant, beautiful but useless, and the attractions of its gardens somewhat played down. Instead we hear of the poverty of the times: "the village children, on the other hand, generally wore the discarded clothes of their parents," and of the frequency of infant mortality: "was it that year that Evie Tomlin died? Later, Stanford people could not remember: it was no unusual thing for a child to die." The inferior status of women is pointed out, and the particular difficulties that women of spirit like Laura have to face, brought up to do nothing but get married. Victor, the schoolmaster's son, does not touch his cap often enough, according to Sir Robert; and Lady Hatton thinks "Simple reading, writing and sums were enough for the Stanford village children, as for their fathers in *her* father's time. More would only make them dissatisfied with their lot." It is best summed up by the stone breaker. When Laura points out that he is doing a useful job, his reply is heavy with a sarcasm that is lost on the children, except for Hugh:

> I'm glad to think that I'm making the stones ready to fill the potholes in the road, so that the carriages won't bump so much. That's bad for the springs of the carriages and for the coachmen and horses and the fine gentry that ride in the carriages.

The Children of the House differs from the other three novels in that there is almost no narrative. The plot consists of a series of incidents — punting, the walk to Honeford, the attempt to see Victor — which are connected only by their being shared by the same four characters; there is no story as *Minnow on the Say* has a story. The author stresses in the Prologue that *The Children of the House* is the story of Laura, Tom, Hugh and Margaret; and as if she wanted to point out that we must not expect a complete narrative with a neat beginning, middle and end, she begins chapter three with:

> In the ordinary course of things, most children do not lead adventurous lives; and the Hatton children were no exception. Their adventures were the ones they made for themselves — deliberately or by accident.

But we never feel that the book is aimlessly episodic; the style of the writing is its great unifier. In no other novel of Philippa Pearce is this more evident or more successful. It reads like one long prose-poem from its melancholic opening sentence "No children live at Stanford Hall now" to its last dying echo, the name "Elsie — Elsie — Elsie" reverberating through the empty rooms.

It seems very unlikely that Philippa Pearce will yield to pressures to write another novel just because her publishers or her readers wish that she would do so. She writes only when she needs to write; her work is an expression of her own feelings and values. One senses behind the text of the books a woman who has suffered a great deal, one whose own childhood was probably unhappy and frustrated. The impression, of course, may be wrong, but one can't help feeling that her peculiar strength and appeal comes from an ability to realize in words — to the point of perfection at times — the sensibility and experience of a very complex and compassionate person. She is one of the great creative artists.

References

PHILIPPA PEARCE

Minnow on the Say Oxford 1955; World 1958 (as *Minnow Leads to Treasure*)
Tom's Midnight Garden Oxford 1958; Lippincott 1959
A Dog So Small Constable 1962; Lippincott 1963
"The Tree in the Meadow" in *What the Neighbours Did* Longman 1972; Crowell 1973

BRIAN FAIRFAX-LUCY AND PHILIPPA PEARCE
The Children of the House Longman 1968; Lippincott
1968

CHARLOTTE BRONTË
Jane Eyre first published in 1847

CHARLES DICKENS
Bleak House first published in 1853

ROBERT WESTALL
The Machine Gunners Macmillan, London, 1975; Greenwillow 1976

ENID BLYTON
Five Go Off in a Caravan Hodder 1947; Atheneum n.d.

PAULA FOX
The Stone-Faced Boy Bradbury 1968; Macmillan,
London 1969

Hanging in
Their True Shapes

♦

ALAN GARNER

JUSTIN WINTLE, in *The Pied Pipers*, suggests that in
Alan Garner "a major talent is energetically destroying
itself; or, more hopefully, it is remarshalling its resources."
It has always seemed to me that Alan Garner is capable of
writing a work of major importance and that *The Owl
Service* and *Red Shift* should have been such works, not
the flawed masterpieces they are. The lines in T. S. Eliot's
"The Hollow Men"—"Between the conception/ And the
creation/ . . . Falls the Shadow" — are very relevant to
Garner's work.

This is not to say that reading his stories is not a
fascinating and absorbing experience. From *The Weirdstone of Brisingamen* to *The Aimer Gate* the technical expertise and the exploration of powerful emotions in areas
where myth and the world of everyday reality meet show
a remarkable development, even if the reader is left unsatisfied in some way or other with every single one of
his books. Garner himself said of *The Weirdstone of
Brisingamen* that he thinks it "is one of the worst books
published in the last twenty years." It depends, of course,
on what criterion is used to define *worst*, but neither it
nor its sequel *The Moon of Gomrath* are particularly
interesting or profound. Both novels are like any hackneyed thriller or TV serial; they merely hold the reader's
attention by placing the good characters in one dangerous
situation after another and then rescuing them. There is
nothing more. Evil is in no way internalized in the charac-

ters, who are either flat, uninteresting figures (Colin and Susan), talking notice-boards issuing instructions or explanations (the wizard and the various dwarfs), or caricatures (Gowther Mossock). Garner's note at the end of *The Moon of Gomrath* that Gowther Mossock is taken straight from life may well be true, but the Cheshire farmer does not come through as anything other than the standard English rustic of fifty or a hundred years ago. The writing in both books is quite adequate, despite some bejeweled and mannered passages, but it is not especially exciting. This extract from *The Moon of Gomrath* is characteristic:

> The notes rose and fell in a sadness that swept the children's minds with dreams of high landscapes of rock, and red mountains standing from them, and hollows filled with water and fading light, and rain drifting as veils over the peaks, and beyond, in the empty distances, a cold gleam on the sea. And into that distance the voice faded like an echo, and Atlendor came towards the children from the shadows of the house.

Why are these novels so unmemorable? The explanation may lie in part in Garner's own comment that he felt "if I could not write for people twice my age, I could perhaps . . . say something which would be of interest to people half my age." In other words, they are written specifically for children, indeed for the child whose major interest in a book is simply what happens next, which is not to say that such books should not exist or should not have an important function in many children's lives. The point is that too many pretentious claims have been made for Garner's first two novels. A study of some of the original reviews is interesting. Of *The Weirdstone of Brisingamen*, the *Sunday* [London] *Times* said it "has a strong, Wagnerian quality"; the *Scotsman* felt it was "one of those grand tales that may be read a hundred years hence as eagerly as it is read now"; the *Manchester Evenings News* called it "absolutely first class." *The Moon of Gomrath* was a book, *The Teacher* claimed, in which "the thoughtful reader could find . . . a fable of our time," and *Books and Bookmen* said, "a timeless story, full of wonder and magic, terror and beauty. A fine author, indeed, and perhaps one of a new generation of classics."

Now, it seems to me that books which offer only conveyed fear and nothing more to interest the reader — whether they have plots wrapped up in a lot of mythological paraphernalia and difficult Celtic names or are science fiction or cops-and-robbers stories — are readable once and once only. They're the equivalent of *Kojak* or *Star Trek*, however well written or well researched. They are not fables of our time or "Wagnerian" or "a new generation of classics."

Elidor, however, shows Garner emerging as a rather more interesting writer than either *The Weirdstone of Brisingamen* or *The Moon of Gomrath* suggested. The plot has greater unity and purpose — we are not merely subjected to a series of disconnected danger sequences — and it is possible for the reader to feel that the story is not aimed just at a certain kind of child. It has something interesting to say, on a number of different levels, about imagination and reality, about the position and importance of myth in a modern context, about the power and significance of place. The derelict church and the cobbled working-class streets of Manchester, with their years of private and public history swept away by the bulldozer in the name of progress, are portrayed convincingly, particularly when paralleled with the blighting of the world of Elidor and contrasted with the security and safety of the Watsons' house, graceless though that house may be. Everyday life may be dull, but it is stable and necessary if the children are to survive; yet if they are to grow up as complete human beings and not become the television-obsessed automata that their parents are, they also need to know Elidor as it once was and realize the importance of restoring it to its former glory, so that it may take its part in their own adult lives, a symbol of the powers of the imaginative and creative life. Only Roland is able to appreciate this fully; for Helen, Nicholas, and David, Elidor will in time probably fade to nothing more than a disturbing memory.

So myth, then, in *Elidor* is a way of expressing certain fundamental truths about human behavior. That is a right and proper function of myth; using it as a glorified cops-and-robbers tale is not. The book has other strengths; the Watson parents, observed with a tolerant amusement, are the first credible characters that Garner created. They are in fact more interesting than the children — who are still cardboard creations as in the previous two books — and the parents show that the author has a talent for social comedy which, unfortunately, he has not employed elsewhere:

> Mrs Watson took the evening paper, and made a point of reading it. Every minute or so she would turn the pages fretfully, as if they were responsible for the television breakdown.

These cardboard children are a problem, the major flaw in the novel. Their speech does not serve to differentiate character, nor does it always sound very realistic; the dialogue could be rearranged so that David could speak Helen's lines, or Helen Nicholas's, and the book would not suffer:

> "Fine," said David. "But how do you get the Treasures into Elidor?"
> "Search me," said Nicholas.
> "Malebron won't have a hope," said Roland.
> "That's his problem," said Nicholas. "We didn't volunteer for this."
> "Nick's right," said David. "We can't hide them, and we can't fight for them."
> "What about the unicorn?" said Helen.

They simply aren't flesh-and-blood people. The closeness of the plot to C. S. Lewis's *The Lion, the Witch, and the*

Wardrobe is uncomfortable. Alan Garner's dislike of Lewis's novels is well-known, yet in *Elidor*, as in the Narnia stories, four rather uninteresting children are taken to lands ruined by the powers of darkness, which need the children to help restore them to their former grandeur. Was Garner attempting to rewrite Lewis, using the same idea for what he thought were better ends? Or was the parallel less conscious? The answer is not clear.

Nor is the ending of *Elidor* particularly clear; it is the first example in Garner's work of an obscurity that bedevils much of the two subsequent books, as if the author were deliberately cloaking himself in a veil of secrecy because he did not seem to want the reader, for some reason, to peer too closely into the sources of what he had to say. Garner's own words about the conclusion of Elidor are not very helpful. "If the book had gone on another page Roland would have gone mad ... When he watches the dying Findhorn (based heavily on Platonic philosophy), it's not the back of the cave he sees when he looks into the creature's eyes, but rather he is in the cave himself: and he sees that in order to achieve another shadow he has killed the reality." I cannot think that any reader, child or adult, would realize that the concepts expressed here form the ending of *Elidor*: madness, Plato, the cave, the shadow — they may be in the author's mind, but they are not there in the words. And in any case, what does Garner's statement mean? It sounds even more obscure than what it is intended to elucidate.

It is *The Owl Service* and *Red Shift*, however, on which Alan Garner's reputation stands, and they are undoubtedly the books for which he would like to be considered a serious and important writer. *The Owl Service* has received an acclaim permitted to few novels. It is the only book — apart from Richard Adams's *Watership Down* — to have been awarded both the Carnegie Medal and the Guardian Award; it has been made into a television serial, found immensely favorable attention from reviewers

and critics, and received what is perhaps ultimate canoniza-
tion in being called by John Rowe Townsend "the most
remarkable single novel to appear on a children's list in
the 1960s"— a judgment with which most people would
concur. It also appears to have been extremely widely read.
Red Shift was treated less kindly, many people finding
its obscurity very nearly impenetrable. This seems rather
odd, as *The Owl Service* presents at least as many problems to the reader as the later book, and, in any case,
subsequent rereadings solve most, though not all, of the
difficulties of both novels. The final puzzle is not that
they are so obscure, but why the author should wish to
try and make them so, a puzzle to which there does not
seem to be an easy answer.

Both books demand an excessively close attention to
nuance, to what is being stated beneath the words, to what
is left out; this requires an intensity of intellectual concen-
tration that is, curiously, at variance with Garner's own
statement that "because I am writing a novel I am primarily in the entertainment business, providing an emotional
experience, not an intellectual one." In fact, there is not
much in either book that is entertaining in the conventional
sense of the word, but there is a great deal to be admired.
The dovetailing of three stories in *Red Shift*, widely
separated in time but linked in theme and in the use of the
same locale, is masterly and satisfying; there is the opportunity, which the author fully employs, for each story
not only to comment obliquely on the other two and thus
underline what he wishes to say, but also to point to
difference and similarity between then and now and to
push the reader into thinking about people in a context
of history even wider than the two thousand years that
separate the first and last stories. In *The Owl Service*,
especially, there is the power of place:

> He saw mountains wherever he looked: nothing but   •   61
> mountains away and away and away, their tops hidden
> sometimes, but mountains with mountains behind them

in desolation for ever. There was nowhere in the world to go.

"Alison —"

He stood, and the wind was cold through him. He looked again, but there was nothing, and the sky dropped lower, hiding the barren distances, crowding the hills with ghosts, then lifting, and he looked again. Nothing.

There is, too, a similar contrasting of the effect of that place and the myth that rules it on different generations of people. And in both books there is the excitement of a totally gripping suspense that works in every re-reading, because it is not so much an external danger as one that exists inside characters who see themselves on the brink of disintegration when confronted by people and events that force their weaknesses to the surface.

The Owl Service, I repeat, is a flawed masterpiece, however, and it has suffered from a generally uncritical adulation that is blind to both its virtues and its defects. Regrettably, it is often studied in the schoolroom; if any book needs to be read whole, and privately, this one does: Read it aloud and ask questions about *The Mabinogion*, and its spell is destroyed. Many people feel that is is a profound and searching study of adolescence; Penelope Farmer has spoken of its influence on her writing, particularly on *Charlotte Sometimes* (an influence, I must confess, I fail to see). If it's really a marvelous portrait of adolescence, then all teenagers must be maimed and tortured: Gwyn, Roger, and Alison are emotional cripples — Gwyn, in fact, says this to Alison — corrupted by their selfish, crippled parents, and they will probably go on to inflict the same patterns on their own children. Not all, not even most, adolescents are like this. Penelope Farmer, in fact, has a much wider and more generous view of that period of life in *A Castle of Bone*, as does Ursula Le Guin in *A Wizard of Earthsea*, which is surely a much more deserving candidate for the accolade of "the most remarkable single novel to appear on a children's list in the 1960s."

Aidan Chambers says he is "amused to observe how difficult the middle-class enclave find the ending [of *The Owl Service*] . . . They say it mars the story and is a weakness when, in fact, it is the book's great strength." The ending is, by any standards, confused and not a strength. The problem Aidan Chambers is referring to is that many readers feel the wrong boy gets the girl, and they may indeed honestly feel that they have been cheated, as they have been asked by the author throughout the book to identify with Gwyn, to be inside his thoughts and feelings, hopes and fears and to regard Roger as insipid, humorless, and repugnant. "She could have had a Heathcliff, but instead she gets a Young Conservative," someone once remarked. The point is that Alison inevitably is not going to find a Heathcliff; she is too trapped and crushed; she can never be herself, as Gwyn so often urges her, dominated as she is by her revolting mother. The reader, by identifying with Gwyn, is lulled into forgetting that he is just as maimed even though he is more sympathetic; he is no Heathcliff and is never likely to be. The ending, then, is surely right intellectually, but it is fair to say that the author should not have asked us to be so much on Gwyn's side emotionally; it leads inevitably to confusion, to a sense of letdown.

Aidan Chambers's remarks point, rightly, to the interesting class tensions in the book, but here again there is weakness, not strength. Gwyn is any working-class boy with a chip on his shoulder that grows to an enormous size when confronted with the closed doors of the moneyed English middle class; he is not really specifically Welsh, despite the author's impeccable handling of the Welsh speech rhythms. And Roger and Clive seem to me as phony as Gwyn's Welshness. They are standard ◆ 63 caricatures of the chinless, witless, public-school type, observed externally with all the inaccuracies and flatness that are characteristic of the outside observer, particularly the frustrated working-class observer. No one ever uses so many stereotyped clichés of speech as Clive does; he really isn't credible. Alison's mother Margaret might make up for this, but unfortunately she doesn't appear at all in person. (In fact she's left to surface as Tom's mother in *Red Shift* in all her totally credible nastiness, changed though she is into a working-class woman.) Margaret's absence is interesting; and Alan Garner's own views about this seem a weak justification for the device: "I was half way through the book before I realized she hadn't [appeared]. I thought, 'Now why hasn't she? I wonder if it works if she doesn't? . . . I wouldn't have kept it that way if I thought it hadn't.' " I don't think it does work; why her? one asks. It's so arbitrary. Why not leave out Nancy or Clive or even Gwyn? It is a hole, an unnecessary one; and the trouble is that without Margaret's presence Roger and Alison seem more unsympathetic than they should be. If we could have seen her effect, in person, on her daughter and stepson we would feel for them more, and the reader's sympathies would not have been tilted so dangerously towards Gwyn, resulting in the unsatisfying cheated feeling at the end.

Another problem, perhaps less important, is what happens to Nancy. Does she walk over the pass to Aberystwyth or literally vanish into thin air, dead? The latter seems more probable, but why? And why isn't it clear? Perhaps one of the reasons for the obscurities in both books derives from the author's method of working. For *The Owl Service* he says, "I put myself on a two-year crash course of Welsh economic history, Welsh political history, geology, geography. I went into Welsh poetry, I learned Welsh," and *Red Shift* involved "nearly seven years of unbroken work" and "a bibliography of something like two hundred books. I got that out of the

way in the first two years. It's like reading for a degree
— that intensity." Yet the actual writing process, he tells
us, is fairly brief, in the case of *The Owl Service* very
brief — twelve weeks. Is it possible that all that Welsh
economic history (its relevance may seem somewhat
marginal), those hundreds of books, got in the way
rather than helped? Garner's statements about his method
of working are curious in another way, too; they are
more like the kind of statement that one of his more
tortured characters might make (Tom in *Red Shift* is
the most likely one) rather than deeply-felt verbalizations
about the creative processes, which have more to do with
a conscious and subconscious linking of the different parts
of a person's experiences and needs than self-conscious
research.

It would perhaps be only repetitive to launch at this
point into a similar analysis of *Red Shift*, for the same
puzzles and dissatisfactions arise to mar its very considerable virtues, especially, once again on the last page.
Do the characters survive or not? What happens to the
relationship between Tom and Jan? Is it over? Is there
hope for any of them, or not? The reader would like to
know. (Decoding the letter doesn't help much, either.)
It is, however, worth saying again that a great number
of the book's difficulties do resolve themselves on a second
or a third reading, and it is also worth pointing out that
the general comment made on its publication — that it is
not a children's book — is unimportant, though it was
perhaps not quite honest of the publishers to place it on
a children's list. It is not a children's book any more or
less than is *The Owl Service*, although some young people
may derive enjoyment from it.

A more fitting conclusion would be to speak of
Alan Garner's most recent work, the quartet of stories
that begins with *The Stone Book*. The last of them, *The
Aimer Gate*, seems to be falling into the old fault of unnecessary obscurity — what *is* the Aimer Gate? one asks —

and the middle two, *Tom Fobble's Day* and *Granny Reardun*, are less good than *The Stone Book*. In this first story, very brief though it is, there are signs that bear out Justin Wintle's view that here is "a major talent . . . remarshalling its resources," whereas *The Owl Service* and *Red Shift* point to that talent "energetically destroying itself." Story line, relationships, tension, underlying significance all marry in total harmony — the conveyed fear in *The Stone Book*, for instance, is Garner's best yet, a scene on a church spire which fills the reader with an appalling sense of vertigo — and it is much to be hoped that this new-found inner harmony will be expressed in a full-length novel in which the shadow does not fall between the conception and the creation. Alan Garner has all too frequently reminded me of one of the castles in his own Elidor, magnificent but ruined, waiting like Roland for "the glories of stone, sword, spear, and cauldron" to hang "in their true shapes." In *The Stone Book* they have begun to hang in their true shapes, and when they do so in a more extended work, they will certainly make a masterpiece worth the reading.

References

ALAN GARNER

The Weirdstone of Brisingamen Collins, London, 1960; Walck 1969

The Moon of Gomrath Collins, London, 1963; Walck 1967

Elidor Collins, London, 1965; Walck 1967

The Owl Service Collins, London, 1967; Walck 1968

Red Shift Collins, London, 1973; Macmillan, New York, 1973

The Stone Book Collins, London, 1976; Collins + World 1978

Tom Fobble's Day Collins, London, 1977; Collins + World 1979

Granny Reardun Collins, London, 1977; Collins + World 1978
The Aimer Gate Collins, London, 1978; Collins + World 1979

JUSTIN WINTLE AND EMMA FISHER
The Pied Pipers Paddington, London, 1975; Paddington, New York, 1975

T. S. ELIOT
"The Hollow Men" first published in 1925

C. S. LEWIS
The Lion, the Witch, and the Wardrobe Geoffrey Bles, 1950; Macmillan, New York, 1950

RICHARD ADAMS
Watership Down Rex Collings 1972; Macmillan, New York, 1975

JOHN ROWE TOWNSEND
A Sense of Story Longman 1971; Lippincott 1971

The Mabinogion

PENELOPE FARMER
Charlotte Sometimes Chatto 1969; Harcourt 1969
A Castle of Bone Chatto 1972; Atheneum 1972

URSULA K. LE GUIN
A Wizard of Earthsea Parnassus 1968; Gollancz 1971

AIDAN CHAMBERS
"Letter from England", *The Horn Book*, October 1976

Alan Garner's own comments about his work are taken from his essay "Coming to Terms" in *Children's literature in education*, July 1970, and from *The Pied Pipers* by Justin Wintle and Emma Fisher.

Timor Mortis
Conturbat Me

◆

E. B. WHITE and
DORIS BUCHANAN SMITH

VICTORIAN WRITERS of children's fiction had no worries about frightening or horrifying their readers, particularly if they felt it encouraged the young to be good. Death is a common subject in their novels and it is sometimes dwelt on quite lingeringly. Of course death seemed closer to the Victorians than it does to us, not only because of the high infant mortality rate, but because the habit of regular church-going made children aware, at least once a week, of graveyards in which quite probably a brother or a sister was buried. The whole business of funerals was not left, as we leave it, to a firm of faceless undertakers; children would see bodies being "laid out" in their own homes. Catherine Storr said, in "Fear and Evil in Children's Books," that "we are much more squeamish than our forebears were." The Victorians, she added, wrote about death with "loving detail," and "they wrote about poverty, brutality, lunacy, feeble-mindedness, alcoholism, gross injustice and various other sordid aspects of life which we would probably hesitate to introduce to children now." With the exception of sex; that is a subject which we can write about in books for young readers, whereas the Victorians left it severely alone.

Death, on the other hand, causes all sorts of problems for us in children's fiction that did not bother them. It is usually an acceptable subject these days in a story for teenagers, though even here there are occasional cries of alarm. Ivan Southall's *Finn's Folly* was greeted by a generally hostile press everywhere, not just because it was a bad novel — and certainly it's overwritten, strains credulity, piles one Grand Guignol effect on top of another — but because it opened with a car crash in which several people were violently killed. It was a book many people thought was irresponsible. Geoff Fox, however, points out in "Growth and Masquerade" that teenage readers disagree with this assessment; they feel that it would be dishonest of Southall to evade the issue of sudden and violent death, which, after all, happens in some place or other every day of the week. I think the teenagers are right. Hundreds of children each year have one or both parents snatched from them in such a way; why shouldn't there be novels which deal with the subject, which may well help the young to come to terms with bereavement? Writers and publishers, it seems to me, consistently underestimate what is "suitable" for children in matters that are frightening and horrifying. We are, as Catherine Storr says, more squeamish than our forebears.

If death is at times a difficult problem in the teenage novel, it is almost completely taboo in books for younger readers, particularly in fiction for seven-to-ten-year-olds where it is conspicuous by its nearly total absence. The one great modern classic about death, however, is, as everyone knows, E. B. White's *Charlotte's Web*. The author plunges us straight into the topic on the first page, no holds barred:

> "Where's Papa going with that ax?" said Fern to her mother as they were setting the table for breakfast.
> "Out to the hoghouse," replied Mrs. Arable. "Some pigs were born last night."
> "I don't see why he needs an ax," continued Fern, who was only eight.
> "Well," said her mother, "one of the pigs is a runt.

It's very small and weak, and it will never amount to anything. So your father has decided to do away with it."

"Do *away* with it?" shrieked Fern. "You mean *kill* it? Just because it's smaller than the others?"

Mr. Arable, of course, isn't the sadistic killer he appears to be here, and the pig, Wilbur, is saved — for the time being: the death sentence hangs over him throughout most of the book. Charlotte, the spider, saves him in the end, but there's no cosy sentimentality about this: she dies herself. It's an interesting risk that White takes, for Charlotte is, after Wilbur, the most important character in the story. We become involved with her, like her, know her as a person. So her death is much sadder than if she had been eliminated in the opening chapter, at a point in the narrative where we were not so involved. She dies as a result of giving birth to five hundred and fourteen baby spiders, and the point that White makes, that death is an inevitable and necessary part of the whole scheme of things, is made acceptable by the emphasis he puts, after Charlotte dies, on the joy and happiness of birth, not only of the spiders, but of all the young animals on the farm. The contrast between these two passages, very close to each other in the text, is striking:

> She never moved again. Next day, as the Ferris wheel was being taken apart and the race horses were being loaded into vans and the entertainers were packing up their belongings and driving away in their trailers, Charlotte died. The Fair Grounds were soon deserted. The sheds and buildings were empty and forlorn. The infield was littered with bottles and trash. Nobody, of the hundreds of people that had visited the Fair, knew that a grey spider had played the most important part of all. No one was with her when she died.

> The snows melted and ran away. The streams and ditches bubbled and chattered with rushing water. A sparrow with a streaky breast arrived and sang. The light strengthened, the mornings came sooner. Almost

> every morning there was another new lamb in the sheep-
> fold. The goose was sitting on nine eggs. The sky
> seemed wider and a warm wind blew. The last remain-
> ing strands of Charlotte's old web floated away and
> vanished.

That "no one was with her when she died" is particularly
chilling, but, by the end of the second quotation, it seems
less so; life continues and there is as much joy as there is
grief. The reference to Charlotte's old web floating away
isn't chilling at all; everything is in fact in its right place.
The resolution of the book is splendid.

But — and it's a very important but — characters in
Charlotte's Web, those who are born and who die in
the story, are talking animals. It used to be said that this
was the only way White could have dealt with his
material, that young children could take the idea of death
when it happened to a talking spider, but not if he had
chosen a human being. This argument, I suppose, is
analogous to another commonly held view of the subject,
that our lives may be devastated by the death of someone
who is close to us, but we remain more or less unmoved
by the sight on our television screen of corpses in Northern Ireland or Cambodia or wherever the world's hot spot
of the moment happens to be. There is a flaw in the
argument, however, when it is applied to E. B. White's
book. Charlotte isn't just a talking spider; she may be a
spider in appearance and in some of her functions such
as web-building, but she speaks and feels and thinks like
a human being. To all intents and purposes she is a
woman, a comfortable middle-aged aunt, indeed to Wilbur
more than that: she's a mother-substitute. Certainly she's
not a remote figure in a faraway place, like a dying baddie
in a Western film or a Nicaraguan rebel, seen on TV,
killed in a civil war. Young children, in reading *Charlotte's
Web*, do experience, therefore, some of the feelings they
might well have if someone dies whom they know
intimately.

In Rumer Godden's *The Diddakoi*, which is a book likely to be read by children of the same age as those who would read *Charlotte's Web*, one of the characters dies: Kizzy's grandmother. But is isn't the central issue, shattering though the death is to Kizzy. The author is concerned with a lot of other things, such as the Romany child's adjustment to a life-style very different from the one she's known; the kindness and antagonism shown by the villagers; the relationship between the Admiral and Miss Brooke, and so on. The impact of the death on the reader is therefore much less strong than is the death of Charlotte, crowded out by other matters; and the event itself is announced in the gentlest possible terms:

> Admiral Twiss had found her late that morning lying underneath the wagon and had guessed at once what had happened. Travellers are laid in the open air when they are dying; they do not like to die inside, not even in their wagons, and Gran was peaceful on the frozen grass with Joe quietly cropping tufts alongside.

Admiral Twiss is softening the blow as much as he can for Kizzy's sake, but one can't help feeling that the author is also, to some extent, sheltering the child reader, even if she doesn't spare Kizzy when Gran's wagon has to be burned:

> They were burning the wagon; as Kizzy watched, the body sank, came away from the wheels and the roof fell in. "But why?" asked Kizzy. "Why?" The words seemed to be wrung out of her.

But maybe it's easier to dwell on a burning wagon than a dying woman.

In *A Taste of Blackberries* by Doris Buchanan Smith, however, we do have a story for young children in which death — sudden and inexplicable — is the main theme, and it is a book in which the characters are not talking animals. It received wide critical acclaim in both the United States and in England when it first appeared, but, interestingly, it does not seem to be a book which librarians and parents hurry to give to their children. As literature, it is not in the same league as *Charlotte's Web*; it doesn't have the perfection of narrative shape that White achieves, nor has it either the distinction of his prose style, the excellence of his dialogue, the subtlety of his humor. (The conversation in *Charlotte's Web* between Mrs. Arable and the doctor is a particularly rich piece of comedy, working in several different ways at once.) After E. B. White's achievement, *A Taste of Blackberries* seems flat, all on one level, and too didactic: the moral of "don't accept lifts from strangers," for example, sticks through the brief thunderstorm episode in glaring capital letters. However, the chief purpose of the book is to write about death in a fashion that young readers can take, and in this Doris Buchanan Smith succeeds admirably.

Jamie, a lively, engaging youngster who is very much the leader of the pack, and best friend of the narrator (it's a first-person story in which the 'I' is inexplicably and irritatingly not given a name), has an allergy to bee stings, but no one knows this. About one third of the way through the story, when the author has given herself enough time and space to establish Jamie's character to the point where we are involved with him and his adventures, he dies — stung by a bee. It seems to the people who witness the event, Mrs. Houser and the children, to be so impossible that they can't take in the information:

> Sure enough, it was Jamie, lying still and pale, with his eyes closed. His mother was even paler. She piled into the back with one of the attendants. The other man hopped into the driver's seat and they sped off with a wail. Mrs. Houser stood in the doorway and everyone was quiet.
>
> "What's the matter?" a voice broke the silence.
>
> "All I know is he got stung."
>
> "Stung? Huh! Look at me. I got stung eleven times!" The speaker began to point out his various swollen spots smeared with soda paste.

"Is he dead?"

"Don't be crazy," I said. "Nobody dies of bee stings."

But dead he is; and the nervous, jerky quality of the writing in this extract — even if "piled" and "hopped" sound jarringly wrong — suggests that deep down they know he is dead, but are unable, for the moment, to admit it.

The rest of the book deals with picking up the pieces and coming to terms. Jamie's friend is stunned: unable to eat, unable to accept his parents' sympathy; for a while unable to cry, he withdraws into himself, nursing his grief like a festering wound. The writing here is direct and honest; that adults don't know the answers any more than children do is a point made quite explicit when he asks Mrs. Mullins why Jamie had to die:

> "Honey, one of the hardest things we have to learn is that some questions do not have answers." I nodded. This made more sense than if she tried to tell me some junk about God needing angels.

God and angels or not, Mrs. Mullins's answer does make sense and what she says is a lesson a child has to learn. The narrator feels guilty, somehow responsible for the death — an excellent touch this: even for adults there is always the feeling of "if I hadn't done this, that wouldn't have happened" and children feel even more keenly a sense of guilt when a marriage breaks up or a parent or a friend dies. It must be my fault, they think; it would not have occurred otherwise.

In *A Taste of Blackberries* the boy goes to the funeral, and well done, too, is the sense of detachment, of unreality that funerals sometimes produce in people, a feeling that is really a part of the symptom of shock:

> A man got up and started talking and reading the Bible. He had some blue stripes in his tie that exactly

> matched the flowers on top of the casket. The matching
> blues held my attention over the droning of his words.

The prose here is deliberately drab and lifeless, almost
like meaningless details observed in a dream, and the
dreamlike state of the narrator's mind is emphasized again
a few lines later:

> There was a quiet shift around me. Everyone was stand-
> ing. Their standing pulled me up too, like reverse
> gravity.

Slowly and quietly things move back to normal. But
the boy does not feel himself on the way to being healed
until he goes to talk to Jamie's mother, something he has
previously been unable to do, so strong is his sense of
guilt. Nothing much is said; he gives her a basket of blackberries and she thanks him. But it's enough:

> "How nice," she said. "I'll bake a pie. And you be sure
> to come slam the door for me now and then."

She understands what he feels and is unable to say, and
he senses this; it's the kind of release he has been needing.
With this touching, delicately handled exchange the story
ends. The pieces have been picked up and mended as far
as is possible.

There is absolutely nothing in this story that a young
child cannot take in, nor is there any reason to suppose
that it would be unduly upsetting — not that we can ever
predict what is likely to upset individual children; they
can absorb disgusting atrocities with surprising ease and
then be terrified by something like the noise of a lavatory
cistern. It is often said that if a youngster is put through
a frightening experience in a book, then there should be
a proper resolution, something to redress the balance so
that the reader is not excessively alarmed. But it's impossible to legislate. The story that upset me as a child
more than any other was a rather silly tale about a haunted   • 75
manor house in which the ghost is unmasked at the end
by some children: he's the butler, dressed up in a sheet,

trying to steal the silver candlesticks. A proper resolution, one might think, but this piece of nonsense terrified me out of my wits in a way that not even the brutalities of *Coral Island* or the evil and horror of blind Pew in *Treasure Island* could manage.

Even so, having said that, I think it's probable that the majority of children reading *A Taste of Blackberries* or having it read to them will be comforted rather than bewildered or frightened. We don't have the same facility for coping with death that previous generations had, and our children need some sort of machinery for helping them to deal with it. *A Taste of Blackberries* is a quite reasonable start, and so, in a different way, is *Charlotte's Web*: at the end of the latter book it would be all too easy for the author, writing about the joys of birth and springtime, to forget Charlotte completely, but, very properly, he puts just a touch of melancholy into his concluding lines:

> Wilbur never forgot Charlotte. Although he loved her children and grandchildren dearly, none of the new spiders ever quite took her place in his heart. She was in a class by herself. It is not often that someone comes along who is a true friend and a good writer. Charlotte was both.

Things can't ever be quite the same as they were, he seems to be saying, whatever good times may come; it would be an insult to the dead to forget them completely, to say that what they did and what they stood for is ultimately of no importance. Again this seems to me to be comforting, not depressing. White is telling the child that he is allowed to mourn; that he is allowed to remember with a certain sadness. So is Doris Buchanan Smith. These two authors are saying things that are necessary, and which help children to cope and to grow.

References

E. B. WHITE
   Charlotte's Web Harper 1952; Hamish Hamilton 1952

DORIS BUCHANAN SMITH
   A Taste of Blackberries Crowell 1973; Heinemann 1975

RUMER GODDEN
   The Diddakoi Macmillan, London, 1972; Viking 1972

IVAN SOUTHALL
   Finn's Folly Angus & Robertson 1969; St. Martin 1969

CATHERINE STORR
   "Fear and Evil in Children's Books" *Children's literature in education*, March, 1970

GEOFF FOX
   "Growth and Masquerade" *Children's literature in education*, November 1971

R. M. BALLANTYNE
   Coral Island first published in 1857

R. L. STEVENSON
   Treasure Island first published in 1883

Earthsea Revisited

◆

URSULA K. LE GUIN

URSULA K. LE GUIN has suggested that the influences on her work of her anthropologist father, A. L. Kroeber, and of her historian husband, Charles Le Guin, have given her a curiosity about people different from one's own kind; an interest in artefacts; an interest in languages; a delight in the idiosyncrasies of various cultures; a sense that time is long while human history is very short — and therefore a sense of kinship across seas and centuries; a love of strangeness and of exactness. It is in precisely these areas that the Earthsea novels are astonishingly rich. She may be writing about imaginary people in imaginary places — indeed heroic, larger-than-life people whose virtues and vices are greater than those of ordinary men and whose deeds have an epic quality one finds in the ancient myths and legends of most nations — but these fictional people and places invoke parallels in the reader's mind not only with other stories and myths, but with historical events, real places, and the cultural practices of a variety of different civilizations, past and present.

The three Earthsea books are almost as rich in suggestion and association as the poetry of T. S. Eliot, though the references are not so literary and are much less difficult to assimilate. Thus the Kargad invasion of Gont reminds the reader of marauding Vikings or the Danish attacks on Saxon England; the selection process of the One Priestess of Atuan is reminiscent of Tibetan monks searching for the new Dalai or Panchen lamas; the meeting of the mages in the Immanent Grove to decide on a new archmage recalls the conclave of cardinals electing a pope; and the sacrifice of the prisoners in the labyrinth under the tombs is an echo of the Greek legend of the Minotaur — Ged here playing the role of Jason and Tenar that of Medea. The Children of the Open Sea are not unlike Tahitians as Cook first saw them; the organization and teaching at the School for Wizards on Roke resembles that of universities like Oxford and Cambridge; and the functions of mages and the archmage are to some extent apostolic and call to mind the traditional duties of Christian priests and bishops.

Similar underlying associations apply also to individual characters. There are many parallels between Ged and Jesus as teacher and healer, and the name by which Ged is known, Sparrowhawk, also has Christ-like connotations, for Christ as a hawk is a comparison that has been made before, most notably in Gerard Manley Hopkins's poem, "The Windhover." Indeed, the lines that emphasize Christ's almost terrifying powers —

> Brute beauty and valour and act, oh, air, pride, plume, here
> Buckle! And the fire that breaks from thee then, a billion
> Times told lovelier, more dangerous, O my chevalier!

— could equally well be true of Ged in the great epic moments of the story, such as when he rescues Arren from the slavers, or leads Tenar out of the tombs, or faces the full might of the powers of anti-life, Cob. Even the names of the central characters tell us something about their roles — Arren/Aaron, high priest; Ged/good (even God?); and Tenar is one letter short of an anagram of "renata," Italian for reborn, as well as suggesting tenacity or the French "tenir," to hold.

The names of the islands and the towns in the Archipelago have the same ability to suggest more than they appear to do on the surface; it is no accident that in the northeast part of Earthsea they have a harsh Nordic

quality — Karego-At, Atnini, Hur-at-Hur — very suitable
to their unpleasant warmongering inhabitants, the Kargads
— whereas in the more indolent softer southwest, the
names are gentler and more euphonious — Wellogy, Lor-
banery, Jessage. Ursula Le Guin points to this herself in
The Farthest Shore in a paragraph memorable for its subtle
rhythms and sound effects:

> "Lorbanery," Sparrowhawk replied, and the soft mean-
> ingless syllables were the last word Arren heard that
> night, so that his dreams of the early night wove them-
> selves about it. He dreamed he was walking in drifts of
> soft, pale-colored stuff, shreds and threads of pink and
> gold and azure, and felt a foolish pleasure; someone told
> him "These are the silkfields of Lorbanery, where it
> never gets dark."

Hort Town with its drug-crazed inhabitants is, in contrast, exotic and frantic, like an Eastern bazaar, Hong
Kong perhaps, and the name of the most popular drug
there is hazia, singularly apt with its suggestion of "haze"
or "daze"; whereas the activity of Gont Port, busy with
selling fish and building ships, seems cleaner and purpose-
ful, more like a harbor in New England or the Western
Isles of Scotland.

Into the complex, detailed background of each novel,
colorful as a tapestry, is woven a story that is bold and
simple in outline, though its meaning is profound and
significant; each has, in fact, a similar story, in which the
forces of good and evil are pitted against each other and
much of the action consists of an exciting chase to find
out the nature of that evil and either defeat it or come to
terms with it. All three novels deal with the fundamental
problems of adolescence — discovering abilities and limitations; acquiring skills; and with the questions: who am I?
what is my place in the world? can I function adequately
and maturely? Ted Hughes, in "Myth and Education,"
argues persuasively that a legend like that of St. George
and the dragon is not the kind of story we should teach

our children; it is damaging and dangerous because the evil (the dragon) is killed: "It sets up as an ideal pattern for dealing with unpleasant or irrational experience the complete suppression of the terror ... It is the symbolic story of creating a neurosis." His own book, *The Iron Giant*, is an attempt to create a myth-like tale that reverses such a situation, and in a much larger way, *A Wizard of Earthsea* does exactly the same thing. The parallels are striking; Ged runs away from the shadow and tries to fight and kill the dragons, just as the farmers attempt to bury the iron giant underground, and in neither case is this action successful. Ged eventually has to confront the shadow, and he also makes a bargain with the dragons: in *The Farthest Shore* he saves them from extinction and Pendor, by taking him and Arren to Havnor, saves Ged's life. So, too, Hogarth comes to terms with the iron giant who stops the space-bat-angel-dragon from devouring the whole world. It seems that Ursula Le Guin, like Ted Hughes, has a contempt for the St. George story: in *The Farthest Shore* dragons are not only left unmolested but they are elevated to a position in the scheme of things that is superior to that of any other beast. Dangerous and unpredictable they may be, but their primitive majesty is awe-inspiring and their wisdom is older than that of man. As Arren says "I do not care what comes after; I have seen the dragons."

Growing up in *A Wizard of Earthsea* is concerned with the recognition, as a basic ingredient of maturity, that evil is within us, is created by us, and has a terrifying independent life of its own unless it is acknowledged and allowed a space in our lives; only then can it be controlled. It cannot be escaped: Ged flees back and forth across the Archipelago trying to avoid it; he's someone "afraid of his own shadow"— but ultimately it has to be faced. He becomes adult only when he discovers that the shadow pursuing him is himself, when he accepts that that is so and can give it room inside himself:

> Ged had neither lost nor won but, naming the shadow of his death with his own name, had made himself whole: a man: who knowing his whole true self, cannot be used or possessed by any power other than himself, and whose life therefore is lived for life's sake and never in the service of ruin, or pain, or hatred, or the dark.

The growth processes in this book are also ones that are traditionally masculine, emphasizing the necessity to acquire physical skills; to participate in a life of action, in doing. There is no contemporary blurring of roles here: and it is not the only aspect of the Earthsea trilogy that suggests a novelist whose values are markedly more old-fashioned than those of most modern writers for children.

There is, for instance, a conservative belief in élitism; Ged and Arren are highly gifted children who need a specialist education that is different from that of most others. They obtain that education, and society is repaid by receiving the benefits that they, as adults, can bestow — benefits they would be unable to confer if Ged had not attended the school on Roke, or if Arren had stayed at home and not accompanied Ged on his voyage. Until Arren meets Ged

> He had never given himself entirely to anything. All had come easy to him, and he had done all easily; it had all been a game, and he had played at loving.

Ursula Le Guin seems to be saying that youth needs the challenges adults can offer and the exacting standards some adults require; there is no truck here with fuzzy modern theories of child-centered learning — of allowing the young to do what they want when they want as the key to producing the whole man.

The relationship between adults and children is unlike that found in most modern children's books. It is loving but firm and it neither gives rewards nor exacts punishments, but most important of all, the adults have wisdom and humility achieved through experience; a purpose in life; standards. The vast majority of parents and

authority figures in today's novels for children are de-
feated, insensitive, ineffectual people who are utterly bewildered by the world about them — you can see it across
the whole spectrum of stories from Philippa Pearce to
Paula Fox, from E. L. Konigsburg to Penelope Farmer,
from Paul Zindel to Alan Garner — characters who have
nothing to give or to pass on other than neurosis and
conflict; whose lack of belief in themselves and anything
outside themselves in many instances imprisons the young
in immaturity, in a specialized youth culture that is the
very reverse of growing up. But in Ursula Le Guin's
novels they do have something to offer the young. They
can teach; Ged can say to Arren:

> An act is not, as some young men think, like a rock
> that one picks up and throws, and it hits or misses,
> and that's the end of it ... But we in so far as we
> have the power . . . must learn to do what the leaf and
> the whale and the wind do of their own nature. We
> must learn to keep the balance. Having choice, we must
> not act without responsibility.

All three novels have a great deal to say about the
necessity for equilibrium, and, in *The Farthest Shore*,
about ecological balance, if man is to survive at all. *The
Farthest Shore*, in fact, is a powerful indictment of the
standards and mores (or rather the lack of them) of contemporary society. It strongly attacks the idea that man
should do things just because he has the capacity to do
them, which leads in real-life to the dead ends of pollution
and poison or white elephants like Concorde or space
mission debris left on the moon. In Earthsea this capacity
leads to an arid quest for immortality that makes people
forget the words and meanings of their songs, makes
wizards forget their spells, and leads eventually to a general
denial that wizardry ever existed. It is clearly a comment
on modern civilized man who has abandoned religion, left
no place in his life for the powers of myth, the supernatural, the unknown. Ted Hughes is again in agreement

with Ursula Le Guin when he says in "Myth and Education" that three hundred years of rational enlightenment and scientifically-biased education have produced a chronically sick, apathetic society, one which is "prohibiting imagination . . . reducing the Bible to a bundle of old women's tales, finally murdering God." Ursula Le Guin, less emotively but just as effectively, says through Ged in *The Farthest Shore*:

> It is much easier for men to act than to refrain from acting... Do nothing because it is righteous or praiseworthy, or noble, to do so; do nothing because it seems good to do so; do only that which you must do, and which you cannot do in any other way.

and, later on, in the same book,

> Would you give up the craft of your hands, and the passion of your heart, and the hunger of your mind, to buy safety?

In these changed circumstances Arren is growing up; the world is not the place it was when Ged was young. The maturing process in *The Farthest Shore* doesn't deal with the recognition of the evil in oneself as it does in *A Wizard of Earthsea*. It is more concerned with the young learning from those older than themselves; with blind hero-worship of a charismatic man which can easily change to its opposite, doubt and fear; but which, as the relationship deepens and goes through a number of shared experiences, can turn into a mutual trust, respect, and affection. It shows, too, that adulthood means belief in oneself and learning not to rely on others. But as in *A Wizard of Earthsea*, there is a traditionally male world of action and doing.

The Tombs of Atuan, however, is quite different in this respect. The central character, Tenar, is a girl, and we see her at first as a prisoner in several senses, not only because she is the One Priestess of the Tombs, devoted to a life of ritualistic mumbo-jumbo and religious ceremonies that have long since ceased to have any real point —

the word that was repeated over and over again was a
word so old it had lost its meaning, like a signpost still
standing when the road is gone

— but because she is also a prisoner of a sterile single-sex
environment in which there is scarcely any affection, let
alone love. Most of all she is trapped inside herself, eaten
up with vindictiveness, hatred, and self-centeredness, with
intellectual cleverness that makes her adept only at petty
back-biting and bitchery. The darkness of the tombs, the
subterranean labyrinth of which she is mistress, her given
name, Arha — a dull, unmusical noise which means "The
Eaten One" — stress the fact that she has never had the
least opportunity to grow as a person. From all this Ged
rescues her; yet more important than that is the capacity
he brings out in her to rescue herself from the worst effects
of her upbringing: he is able to teach her to accept her
femininity as a great source of good rather than evil. *The
Tombs of Atuan*, in having the central relationship one
between male and female, makes very different points
from either *A Wizard of Earthsea* or *The Farthest Shore*,
and the differences are emphasized by the setting of the
book being so static, on land, and mostly underground in
darkness, as opposed to the rapid movement, the color, the
journeys, the daylight of the other two.

Tenar's suppressed vitality has outlets in uncontrolled
aggression, but, once Ged appears in the labyrinth, it is
focused entirely upon him. The interest on her side is
intensely sexual, and the reader, watching Ged through
her eyes, sees him in a way that was not possible in *A
Wizard of Earthsea*: as a physically beautiful man, a potential lover or husband. The appearance of his body
is frequently mentioned — his long hands "copper brown
and quiet on his knees," his voice "deep and resonant";
he's observed standing with one hand on his hip, "the
other holding out at an angle the wooden staff as tall as
he was." Tenar's discovery that this attraction can bring
her freedom, not only from the tombs but from every-

thing else that has stunted her, is the main theme of the book, the real climax coming not so much in the excitement of the earthquake destroying the tombs, but in the joining of the two halves of the ring of Erreth-Akbe, symbolizing, among other things, a spiritual and emotional union between her and Ged. But freedom, she learns, is a "heavy load," however preferable it may be to her life in the tombs:

> It is not easy. It is not a gift given, but a choice made, and the choice may be a hard one. The road goes upward towards the light; but the laden traveler may never reach the end of it.

In discussing the themes dealing with adolescence in the Earthsea novels rather than the mythology, I am interested, like some of the characters, with restoring balance and equilibrium. Ursula Le Guin has, more than most children's authors, received attention from people who are not normally readers of children's literature, and that, I suspect, is because she is a writer of myth. A children's book that has the appearance of myth seems, oddly, to be much more acceptable to many adults than a fantasy or a realistic novel. This can be seen in the enthusiasm for Alan Garner; in the cult of rather second-rate authors like C. S. Lewis or Tolkien; or in the colossal sales of Richard Adams's long-winded and utterly humorless — if anthropologically impeccable — rabbit saga, *Watership Down*. Philippa Pearce and Paula Fox, who don't write myth but whose qualities as creative artists are second to none, are studiously ignored. As far as Ursula Le Guin is concerned, probably enough has been written about the mythological aspects of the Earthsea books and the parallels with her works of science fiction; but it has not been sufficiently pointed out that as a writer for and about teenagers she is in the front rank. Almost everything that the teenage problem novel deals with in a realistic fashion is dealt with in the Earthsea trilogy, and both the depiction of the teenagers themselves and the answers Ursula Le Guin gives to the problems of growing up are refreshingly different from what one is likely to find in almost any other novels for adolescents. Nor is it just a matter of talking about current difficulties or crazes; she is unusual in that she isn't afraid to emphasize, in *The Farthest Shore*, what she thinks the preoccupations of the young *ought* to be:

> When I was young I had to choose between the life of being and the life of doing. And I leapt at the latter like a trout to a fly. But each deed you do, each act, binds you to itself and to its consequences, and makes you act again, and yet again. Then very seldom do you come upon a space, a time like this, between act and act, when you may stop and simply be. Or wonder who, after all, you are.

Perhaps our craving for myth comes from our loss, long ago, of our tribal singers and poets, and the mythic world created by Tolkien, for example, seems, therefore, like drink to a man dying of thirst — just as the intense desire expressed by vast numbers of people to live in a country cottage with roses round the door is not just a distaste for metropolitan life, but another awareness of loss, a yearning for our long-dead rural roots. The Earthsea books put us in touch with those roots; there is probably more in them, much much more, that is concerned with the world of nature than with the world of myth. And here it is balance once again that is constantly brought to our attention: the contrast of opposites, the equilibrium nature has attained that man is destroying but which he must strive to preserve. So the fountain glittering in the sunlight of Roke's courtyard is set against the spider's web the Master Patterner observes in the Immanent Grove; the otak makes a splendid pet for Ged but it has cruel teeth and a vicious temper; or as the Master Changer says in *A Wizard of Earthsea* "to light a candle is to cast a shadow," and Ged in *The Tombs of Atuan*:

> The earth is beautiful and bright and kindly, but that

is not all. The earth is terrible and dark and cruel. The
rabbit shrieks, dying in the green meadows. The mountains clench their great hands full of hidden fire. There
are sharks in the sea and cruelty in the eyes of men.

The author's observation of the natural world is not, however, confined to these broad strokes. There is a wealth of
minute detail about birds and plants and fish; of concern
with simple craftsmanship like boat-building; of vivid descriptions of seascapes and mountains, fields and deserts,
rain and snow. Man in harmony with nature; man destroying it: Ursula Le Guin's philosophy is not only conservative but deeply conservationist. Magic and wizardry,
in fact, have only a small role to play in the books. Her
own comment on this, in "Dreams Must Explain Themselves," suggests perhaps surprisingly that it isn't anything
to do with the usual place magic has in myth; that it is
not to be seen as one of the conventional attributes of a
superman or a super-hero:

> Wizardry is artistry. The trilogy is then, in this sense
> about art, the creative experience, the creative process.

Ged, as a mature man, never uses magic to show off, to
perform tricks to please an audience; nor does he employ
it as a device to lessen the ordinary hardships of life. Thus
he endures wind and rain in an open boat, to Arren's initial
amazement and annoyance, and will not cast a spell to
create sunshine; rain and wind have necessary functions,
he explains, and if he is to thwart those functions he has to
be fully aware of the consequences of doing so. And he
tells Arren when they are both hungry that he could
easily conjure up a superb meal, but it would only titillate
the senses, not satisfy the appetite. Magic is used in times
of acute difficulty and even then it doesn't always work.
It is symbolic of the inner strengths and reserves a man
88 ♦ has in a real crisis — those strengths with which he can
surprise even himself, because, normally, he is not aware
of their existence. To see wizardry as artistry, as Ursula

Le Guin has said, is to make a comment about literature itself. It is an acknowledgment that books cast a spell, and have the power to turn the reader into the hero of the tale for as long as the story lasts and perhaps even longer; that they are, particularly for the young, a means of experiencing actions and emotional and rational processes which cannot yet be experienced in real life. It is an acknowledgment, above all, that there is some kind of magic about all literature, perhaps in novels in particular, and that the magic is potent, beneficial — and dangerous.

A Wizard of Earthsea, *The Tombs of Atuan*, and *The Farthest Shore* are, in this sense, magic and artistry of an exceptionally powerful nature; the products of a wizard who is truly beneficial, herself an archmage. They return us, as Eleanor Cameron says, "to ourselves, to our own struggles and aspirations, to the very core of human responsibility."

References

URSULA K. LE GUIN

A Wizard of Earthsea Parnassus 1968; Gollancz 1971
The Tombs of Atuan Atheneum 1971; Gollancz 1972
The Farthest Shore Atheneum 1972; Gollancz 1973
"Dreams Must Explain Themselves" Signal, January 1976

GERARD MANLEY HOPKINS

"The Windhover" written 1877; first published 1918

TED HUGHES

"Myth and Education" Children's literature in education, March 1970
The Iron Man Faber 1968; Harper 1968 (as The Iron Giant)

RICHARD ADAMS

Watership Down Rex Collings 1972; Macmillan, New York, 1975

ELEANOR CAMERON

"High Fantasy: A Wizard of Earthsea" The Horn Book Magazine, April 1971

◆ 89

Middle of the Way

◆

RODIE SUDBERY and
BEVERLY CLEARY

THE WRITERS of children's fiction who receive most
critical attention are those who could reasonably be described as "highbrow"; in other words, their books often
have a complexity of style and narrative, a striking originality, or an unusualness of message that appeals in particular to those adults who read children's literature.
While it is probably true that no one has yet produced
a novel for children that is lavishly praised by the pundits
and is totally ignored by the young, it has to be admitted
that much of the work of Alan Garner, Paula Fox, and
others is not read by the great mass of children who do
read for pleasure; the difficulties of style or content make
such writers a minority taste. There is no need to complain
about that: the reading public doesn't often hold up its
hands in horror because Harold Robbins sells more books
than Saul Bellow or John Updike.

It is worth pointing out, however, that there are a
large number of highly competent novelists writing for
the young who don't begin to aim for the heights of a
Philippa Pearce, who are popular with children, yet who
are rarely considered worthy of critical comment. Such
authors may not have great individuality of style nor extreme originality in what they have to say, but they are,
at their best, excellent in their ability to tell a story so
that the young reader is absorbed from beginning to end.
Such writers are Rodie Sudbery, author of a dozen or
more books published in Great Britain; and, in America,

authors like Marilyn Sachs, Isabelle Holland, and Beverly Cleary.

Almost nothing has been written about Rodie Sudbery apart from generally favorable notices when a new novel of hers appears; only one of her books has been published in the United States, and, at the moment, not one is available in England in paperback. But children read them; they are constantly borrowed from libraries; and even the most casual glance at the pages of them would reveal that here is no producer of pulp fiction, no Enid Blyton, no writer of Nancy Drew stories, but someone whose craftsmanship is so good that it is, at its best, a model of its kind.

She frequently uses for her plots the familiar themes children like and feel at home with. *Cowls*, for instance, is concerned with a supposedly haunted house in which the phantom friar is eventually found to be a boy dressed in a duffle-coat; in *Lightning Cliff* the children unmask a thief who has robbed a chocolate warehouse before the police realize his identity; *The Pigsleg* is about a game of dares that gets out of hand; *The House in the Wood* ends with the discovery of buried treasure. One's initial reaction is, perhaps, to say that this kind of material has been done to death; however, in each case, the idea is not only made to seem very plausible, but it is in fact given an individual twist, a new slant. The treasure in *The House in the Wood* is not something the children can keep and live on happily for the rest of their lives; it's a chest full of pound notes buried at the bottom of a lake, and as they handle the money it disintegrates, rotten with years of wet. It's worthless. The characters in *Lightning Cliff* are not seen as clever little so-and-sos, smarter than the police or the crooks; they're a rather badly behaved bunch who disobey their grandparents, annoy the neighbors, and destroy the wall of a field. Their success in finding out the thief's identity is accidental rather than due to their superior intelligence, and at the end of the story they receive —

quite justifiably — more brickbats than rewards for their efforts. And in *Cowls*, the boy responsible for the haunting is not seen as more reprehensible than the other children: the house, empty though it is, does not belong to any of their families, and the troubles they all suffer are a consequence of breaking into property that isn't theirs.

Edward Blishen's comment in *The Guardian* that in *Lightning Cliff* "Rodie Sudbery displays her usual quiet, precise understanding of the minute-by-minute undramatic drama of children's lives" is correct, but it also implies that there is something dull and unexciting about her work, which is in fact far from the truth. Certainly her stories all revolve round quiet, stable middle-class families, with happy undemanding parent-child relationships, where the central character is often unadventurous, indeed insipid — Guy in *The Silk and The Skin* and Paul in *The Pigsleg* are good examples — and in which the ordinary minutiae of children's lives are lovingly recorded; but there is no dullness, no lack of excitement. *The Silk and The Skin* is also an absorbing and at times very nasty exercise in the macabre, a sort of juvenile *Dracula*, in which a group of children dabble in black magic and resurrect the pet of a dead sorcerer, a bat with a violent temper and a talent for wholesale destruction. Worse, it now becomes the pet of a mongoloid child, whose personality, as the tale proceeds, is gradually taken over by the bat; this seven-year-old develops characteristics of such extreme viciousness that it takes the ingenuity of all the other children to bring matters to a halt before some irreversible damage is done. This is not exactly an undramatic scenario, and it is handled with considerable skill.

Few writers, except for Ivy Compton Burnett, use dialogue so frequently as Rodie Sudbery, and one is also reminded of that novelist in other ways: there is a gently mocking sense of humor, and often a touch of acid in the author's comments. A good example occurs in *Cowls*:

> The weather was warm but close, and he trailed lethar-

gically from shop to shop, eyeing her purchases through a haze of boredom. Meals were things that appeared on tables to Frederick; he had no interest in their raw materials.

And in *The Pigsleg*:

> Mrs. Eaglethorpe was large and tweedy. "My dear boy, *hallo*," she said to Paul. "I was *so* sorry to hear of your accident." He wondered which accident she meant until her next words made it clear. "Such a disappointment for you when you were expecting some decent walking with your friends to find yourself in Cambridge with a lot of little girls!"
>
> "Oh I don't mind," he said truthfully.
>
> "I hear you're *marvellous* with them. Now you know Susan of course, and I gather you had a brief encounter with my husband when he took you for an intruder — I *do* hope you didn't find it too offputting?"
>
> "No."
>
> "Oh, good. Unfortunately he had to be out this afternoon, but here's Keith who's just your age and *longing* to meet you — do you play croquet by the way?"

The whole character of the overpowering Mrs. Eaglethorpe is, therefore, suggested by the way she speaks; no other description is necessary.

The Pigsleg is probably her best book. It's a brief masterpiece of neat construction in which the relationships between four families (seven adults and nine children) are explored without ever once leaving the reader in any confusion about who is who, or feeling that any of the characters are unnecessary or ignored. This is no mean technical feat. The characters are sharply individualized in tiny visual pictures that stay in the mind: Mrs. Coplink is first seen in a very ancient raincoat and Wellington boots feeding a goat; Doctor Worsley cycles so fast that his jacket streams out behind him horizontally; Doctor Coplink is observed at a swimming pool, "a tall thin balding man with sandy hair and sandy skin": • 93

Paul couldn't take his eyes off Dr. Coplink's knees; they were the boniest he had ever seen. He wondered if one or two instruments could have been inserted under the skin in the interests of science. Pedometers perhaps, or blood pressure gauges.

The theme of the book is the cutting down to size of Cressida, the delightful but intolerably bossy leader of a gang of children whose parents are all university lecturers. The gang exists, apparently to indulge in ever more dangerous "dares," but in fact for the self-gratification of Cressida. When the dares begin to involve stealing, and the punishment of one of the gang members by the others (Sophy Anne is dared not to speak for a year and proceeds to try and keep totally silent), a great deal of trouble ensues with the adults, particularly with Sophy Anne's mother, the unpleasant Mrs. Blessington, and Cressida is eventually brought under control. It's an extremely funny book with a very satisfying narrative shape; it's much enjoyed by children, but quite unjustifiably neglected by the critics.

Five of Rodie Sudbery's books have the same central character, Polly Devenish. In the first, *The House in the Wood*, she is twelve — an over-imaginative, starry-eyed, bookish child, prone to seeing ghosts of tyrannical father-figures maltreating servants in the attics of old houses; and in the last she is eighteen, a first-year student at York, a young woman of poise, humor, and good sense. The first three novels — *Cowls* is the second and *Rich and Famous and Bad* the third — are undoubtedly more successful than the last two, *Warts and All* and *Ducks and Drakes*. As Polly moves out of childhood into adolescence, Rodie Sudbery's usual skills begin to desert her. The taut narrative of the first three is abandoned for a looser framework in which there is very little story as such, and the reader is left with a rather unsatisfied feeling, as if the author was continually searching for something to write about and not finding it. She shows an inability, too, to handle the complexities of relationships between teenagers of the opposite sex; the adolescent boys in particular seem cardboard thin — vague, feminine creations — and dated: they behave more like teenagers of the nineteen-fifties than those of the present day.

Of the other novels, *A Curious Place* is particularly worthy of comment. It is set in Scotland, and is concerned with the difficulties a middle-class English family from Lincolnshire have to face when they move to the thoroughly alien working-class city of Glasgow, "a curious place" with customs, dialect, a whole way of existence quite unlike their own. The book shows, therefore, an aspect of life in Britain that remains surprisingly untouched in children's books — the enormous regional differences which, despite our mobility and sophisticated means of communication, still exist. Glasgow, in *A Curious Place*, is observed entirely through the eyes of a boy from the English midlands, and it seems unfriendly, threatening, and hideous:

> The road sloped up between trees until they came into the open just where Philip had hoped they would be, across the valley from their flat. It was even more impossible to pick out which was theirs from here. Between them lay the railroad cutting, deep and wide; then the canal, then the towpath, then the old railway. Lines of houses rose one behind the other up the far hill, their road and the road beyond it and the road beyond that, all the way to the top. They made stripes, paler and paler as they receded. Did the dirt come from the railway, wondered Philip, or the gasworks? Their own block was very dark indeed.

Mrs. Grey says that "everything's filthy"; Philip finds "the echoing stone steps and tiled walls" that lead to their flat have "a cold institutional feel"; even the dust lorries are "slightly sinister if you didn't know what they were: there might be anything inside."

The story is mostly about Philip's problems at school:

as a shy, soft-spoken English boy with a strange accent and a different vocabulary he is an obvious victim for the tougher, urban Scottish kids to bully. At first he tries to wheedle his way into the gang by attempting to please everybody (a theme Rodie Sudbery used again in *The Silk and The Skin*), but when this fails, the others turn on him, and for a whole day, he is hunted down like a rat being chased by a pack of dogs. The book ends on a note of cautious optimism; Philip is befriended by another loner, and the gang, who by now grudgingly admire his ability to survive their attacks, decide to leave him in peace, though they are still very far from accepting him as one of themselves. Glasgow, too, is eventually seen not so much as hostile but simply different; and there is a suggestion that were the situation reversed — an urban Glaswegian boy trying to come to terms with rural Lincolnshire — the problems would be very similar. *A Curious Place* is a striking and effective novel, and stresses the fact that our present-day mobility doesn't lessen the feelings of alienation experienced by children when they have to settle far from their roots. It also makes an oblique comment on those books by Rodie Sudbery which show the reverse of disorientation and displacement, suggesting that the middle-class comfort and stability of the Polly Devenish stories, for instance, is a frail thing.

The novels of Marilyn Sachs and Isabelle Holland are not very well known in England, largely because not enough of them have been published there. Of those that have, Isabelle Holland's *Journey for Three* and Marilyn Sach's *Dorrie's Book* and *A Pocket Full of Seeds* are good examples of narrative skill, stories that do not demand too much from the "middlebrow" child, and they are, all three, notable for their originality. *A Pocket Full of Seeds* deals with the plight of the Jews in occupied France at the end of the Second World War, not a common subject for a children's book. Not only does the reader learn some interesting and almost forgotten details of that period of history — that, of all the conquered nations, France was the one most divided against itself; a country where collaborators and resistance fought against each other with great ferocity — but the loneliness, heart-ache, and hardship of a girl separated from the rest of her family in those troubled times are written about with delicacy and poignancy. The last pages are courageous: no happy reunion for Nicole with her parents and sister, but nagging fears that she will never see them again, which is probably more truthful than a contrived happy ending. *Dorrie's Book* belongs more firmly to a common enough American tradition in contemporary children's novels, as it is a first-person narration by a smart-aleck kid and is fashionably concerned with pregnancies and miscarriages; but feelings that this is all derivative stuff disappear when Dorrie's mother gives birth to triplets. The emphasis placed on the family's reactions — that this event is calamitous rather than joyful — is an honest appraisal of the situation. So is Dorrie's jealousy of her siblings; and particularly accurate are the descriptions of the drudgery, the sheer hard work involved in coping with three tiny babies. The last chapters are weak, however: the O'Briens' adoption of the deserted children next door is sentimental and unrealistic, and the fact that Dorrie does not know how to finish off her account of things seems to suggest that the author is also unsure how the book should end.

One isn't asked in Isabelle Holland's *Journey for Three* to take the story very seriously; it's so wildly improbable — three bizarre orphans turning up at the house of a celebrated but bad-tempered author of children's books and demanding to be adopted — that it belongs, despite its apparent realism, to the genre of fantasy. That doesn't matter: the reader knows from the outset that it could not actually happen and that Isabelle Holland is asking him to look for verisimilitude in areas other than the narrative. The relationship between the bearish Nicholas MacBain and Alison, the most engaging of the children, is psychologically truthful, and Alison's attempts to soften MacBain's character are persuasive. When the two unite against the prurient and nosy neighbors the result is extremely amusing and exactly the right way the plot should go. The happy ending is also correct in this larger-than-life sort of story. *Journey for Three* is an excellent example of the well-written, undemanding, escapist literature children frequently need, and it is far above the mundane level of pulp fiction.

The best of these "middle of the road" writers is Beverly Cleary. Her books are, of course, well known and widely read, but it is only in recent years that England has caught up with her; *Beezus and Ramona*, for instance, was published in America in 1955, but it took twenty-three years for it to find itself in a British edition. And it is only in recent years, too, that critics have realized what has always been obvious: that Beverly Cleary is a marvelous writer. A superficial reading of the Ramona stories might suggest formula books and second-hand material: the adventures of a standard naughty little child who is far too boisterous and imaginative for her placid middle-class family and school, each chapter of each book concerning one self-contained incident that follows the same pattern — Ramona upsetting the Hallowe'en plans or the nativity play preparations, or ruining her mother's cooking or her sister's property or her teacher's lessons — an American version of Dorothy Edwards's *My Naughty Little Sister* or Richmal Crompton's *Just William* stories. But a judgment of this sort ignores the number of different ways in which the Ramona books work, the subtle shape of the narrative, and the distinction of the author's wit.

Beverly Cleary writes for varying levels of response, and this reflects an immense skill. Obviously the novels are of interest to the young child of Ramona's age, but they also give the appearance of looking back to that age from an older child's (sister Beezus) point of view, and, on a third level, one is constantly aware of an adult writing about children — for adults as well as children. These three quite different viewpoints are combined — concealed might be a better word — not only in every chapter, but in nearly every paragraph, sometimes in a single sentence. An excellent example of this occurs in *Ramona the Pest*, when Ramona, thrilled that she is wearing a fearsomely ugly witch's costume for the Hallowe'en parade, suddenly becomes frightened because nobody recognizes her. It's worth quoting the passage in full:

> "Ooh, what a scary witch!" said Miss Binney, rather absentmindedly, Ramona thought. Plainly Miss Binney was not really frightened . . . Ramona was. Miss Binney did not know who this witch was. Nobody knew who Ramona was, and if nobody knew who she was, she wasn't anybody.
>
> "Get out of the way, old witch!" Eric R. yelled at Ramona. He did not say, Get out of the way, Ramona.
>
> Ramona could not remember a time when there was not someone near who knew who she was. Even last Hallowe'en, when she dressed up as a ghost and went trick-or-treating with Beezus and the older boys and girls, everyone seemed to know who she was. "I can guess who this little ghost is," the neighbors said, as they dropped a miniature candy bar or a handful of peanuts into her paper bag. And now, with so many witches running around and still more witches on the big playground, no one knew who she was.
>
> "Davy, guess who I am!" yelled Ramona. . . .
>
> "You're just another old witch," answered Davy.
>
> The feeling was the scariest Ramona had ever experienced. She felt lost inside her costume. She wondered if her mother would know which witch was which and the thought that her own mother might not know her frightened Ramona even more. What if her mother forgot her? What if everyone in the whole world forgot her? With that terrifying thought Ramona snatched off her mask, and although its ugliness was no longer the most frightening thing about it, she rolled it up so she would not have to look at it.

The simplicity of the sentence structure and the frequent repetition of ideas show that this kind of writing can be grasped by the young child, but the vocabulary — "miniature," "absentmindedly," "which witch was which," and the reference to trick-or-treating with Beezus — hold the interest of older children (they can regard with amusement the time when they did these things), while the main point being made — that wearing a mask causes a sense of loss of identity — is an ageless concept, experienced by adults as well as children.

The humor also works on the same three levels. Ramona's ingenuity — making stilts out of coffee tins and clanking around the block, singing at the top of her voice, or her literal interpretation of her sister's suggestion that she play Hansel and Gretel (she puts her doll in the oven and inadvertently ruins Beezus's birthday cake) — will doubtless entertain younger children, while her mistakes — thinking "the dawn's early light," for instance, is a dawnzer lee-light, a kind of lamp — will amuse older readers. And there is an adult humor too; when Mrs. Quimby and Mrs. Kemp give their children endless advice about being careful in the traffic, "Ramona and Howie, weighed down by the responsibility of walking themselves to school, trudged off down the street." And sometimes all three come together; the episode in *Ramona and her Father* when Ramona is bewildered by the sight of three girls dressing up for the nativity play is a good example:

> "Are you Jesus's aunts?" she asked.
> The girls found the question funny. "No," answered one. "We're the Three Wise Persons."
> Ramona was puzzled. "I thought they were supposed to be wise *men*," she said.
> "The boys backed out at the last minute," explained the girl with the blackest eyebrows. "Mrs Russo said women can be wise too, so tonight we are the Three Wise Persons."

The use of the word "Persons" and "Mrs. Russo said

women can be wise too" are neat bits of satire, well above the heads of eight-year-olds, but, no matter — they will still be laughing at the remark about Jesus's aunts.

Nancy Chambers's comment in *Signal* on Judy Blume, that "she can encapsulate an emotion or a perception in a single sentence that makes the reader know it for himself as well as knowing it for the character in the book," and Lance Salway's agreement that Judy Blume "really does know how children feel and think and react," seem much more applicable to Beverly Cleary than to Judy Blume. Again and again the adult reader finds himself agreeing with the accuracy Beverly Cleary shows in her portrayal of her characters' feelings and thought processes, particularly in children's mistaken assumptions about what they only half-understand: Ramona thinking that a truant officer is something like a dog catcher and that he will take naughty children away just as the dog catcher took "an elderly overweight Basset hound" from the school playground; "he shut the dog in the back of his truck and drove away with it." There is the same insight when adults underestimate what children feel — Mr. Quimby trying to soothe Ramona when the cat has eaten the Hallowe'en pumpkin, not realizing that she is upset because he is smoking too much, that she's worried "his lungs will turn black." And in the absurd fears children experience, often so absurd that adults just don't understand the strength of the emotions involved: in *Ramona the Brave* Ramona has her own room at last; she no longer has to suffer the irritations of sharing with Beezus; it's something she has looked forward to for months. But she had not realized how frightened she would be, lying in bed, alone in the dark. She dare not tell her parents in case she loses the privileges and status of having a room of her own, and they never discover how terrified she is. She diverts their suspicions by making them think she is afraid of a picture of a gorilla.

Most children love a series of books about the same

characters, but they rarely appeal to adults, the reason probably being that the first of a series is usually the best and its success has prompted the author into writing sequels that don't always match up to the inspiration of the original story. But the opposite, fortunately, is true of Beverly Cleary. The first of the Ramona books, *Beezus and Ramona*, is the weakest, the least amusing, with a final chapter that is a bit too cozy and cloying, but after that she never puts a foot wrong; the invention in its successors never flags and the wit and the narrative skill are always first-rate. This is a rare ability; Rodie Sudbery, for instance, despite the excellence of much of the writing in the Polly Devenish stories, does not, as I've already said, achieve the same consistency.

The appeal of Rodie Sudbery's and Beverly Cleary's work will be chiefly to those children who are readers, but who want something less intellectually demanding than the literature that usually claims most of the experts' attention. Books like theirs not only have an obviously useful function for the young, but they should also be read by adults. The attitude of many people to children's literature — indifference, condescension, ignorance — is ironically referred to by Rodie Sudbery herself in *Ducks and Drakes*, when Penelope Batts spends a lonely Sunday in her first term at York reading a children's book:

> She had been delighted to find that the university book-shop stocked Puffins; she bought them quite frequently, her guilt at such self-indulgence tempered by a feeling that it was the kind of eccentricity expected of students.

The opinion that adult readers of juvenile fiction are self-indulgent or eccentric is widespread, but such an opinion also seems to imply that childhood itself it probably self-indulgent and eccentric, or at the very least a period of life to get through and abandon, not keep in touch with. It's an insult to children's literature of course, but it's also extremely dangerous: it prevents people from being sane, whole human beings.

References

Rodie Sudbery
  The House in the Wood Deutsch 1968; Dutton 1970 (as
  The Sound of Crying)
  Cowls Deutsch 1969
  Rich and Famous and Bad Deutsch 1970
  The Pigsleg Deutsch 1971
  Warts and All Deutsch 1972
  A Curious Place Deutsch 1973
  Ducks and Drakes Deutsch 1975
  Lightning Cliff Deutsch 1975
  The Silk and the Skin Deutsch 1976

Edward Blishen
  review in *The Guardian* of *Lightning Cliff* 1975

Isabelle Holland
  Journey for Three Houghton Mifflin 1975; Macdonald
  1978

Marilyn Sachs
  A Pocket Full of Seeds Doubleday 1973; Macdonald 1978
  Dorrie's Book Doubleday 1975; Macdonald 1976

Dorothy Edwards
  My Naughty Little Sister Methuen, London, 1952

Richmal Crompton
  Just William Newnes 1922

Beverly Cleary
  Beezus and Ramona Morrow 1955; Hamish Hamilton
  1978
  Ramona the Pest Morrow 1968; Hamish Hamilton 1974
  Ramona the Brave Morrow 1975; Hamish Hamilton 1975
  Ramona and her Father Morrow 1977; Hamish Hamilton
  1977

Lance Salway/Nancy Chambers
  "Book Post" *Signal* September 1979

The Color of Skin

◆

MILDRED TAYLOR

MOST CHILDREN at some time or another have to sort
out their feelings about the clashes of their own culture
and upbringing with the values of another type of society
that is very different from theirs, but, in Britain, there
are few good novels for children which deal with such
things in contemporary terms, especially in the highly
sensitive area of the color of one's skin. Many British
writers seem to deal with the problem by a kind of
analogy, by suggesting parallels in a historical context.
One thinks of those stories of Rosemary Sutcliff, for example, set in Roman or Norman Britain, where the uneasy relationships between a conquered people and their
conquerors make interesting comparisons with the rifts
and flashpoints in modern British society, even if the
actual question of emotional reaction to color does not
arise. Indeed, her work sometimes seems to pinpoint irrational prejudice, feelings of superiority or inferiority, more
accurately than children's books such as Nina Bawden's
On the Run and *The Robbers*, Fay Sampson's *F67* or
Naomi Mitchison's *Sunrise Tomorrow*, which have a contemporary setting and a cast of characters who are both
black and white. The finest example, however, of the
historical analogy is by an American writer — *The Slave
Dancer* by Paula Fox.

American authors are more willing to take the bull
by the horns. In *Jazz Country* by Nat Hentoff, Tom, the
sixteen-year-old white hero, son of a well-to-do lawyer,
finds his liberal attitudes to color are hopelessly naive and
inadequate when he becomes friendly with a group of

black jazz musicians. It is not an especially good novel because the writer's somewhat didactic intentions never become properly realized in believable flesh-and-blood characters, but there are one or two scenes that make strong points. At one stage in the book Tom is talking to Danny, the black trumpeter, in a deserted garage; their conversation is interrupted by a policeman who suspects that they have drugs hidden in their clothing:

> "Hey," I said, "you can't search us just like that. We haven't done anything. You're infringing on our civil liberties. My father's a lawyer — " The billy hit me in the stomach and I doubled over.
> "That's one for civil liberties," said the cop. "You got any other advice for me?"

Tom soon learns from incidents like this why the blacks are so bitter, and he begins to take a more mature look at his own fuzzy liberal notions.

Maybe what has been lacking up till now, in England at least, has been a major contribution to children's literature from black writers themselves, and there are doubtless some very good socio-political explanations for this. No amount of books written by white people, however sensitive their portrayal of non-white characters may be, can ever hope to give the reader any real idea of what it is like to be black in a crowded modern American or British urban environment. But Farrukh Dhondy, an Indian who lives in London, does manage, in *East End at Your Feet* and *The Siege of Babylon*, to do just this, and one of the reasons for his success is that, being non-white himself, he is able to present vividly some of the complexities of race relations that often escape the notice of white authors of children's books. Rupert, the West Indian boy in *The Siege of Babylon*, has had twenty jobs since leaving school; "six months ago, he would have been down on the Portobello Road selling second-hand macs and coats." Now he's involved in a futile kidnap attempt which will send him to prison. The downhill path of bad housing, poor

education, and lack of opportunity is made very clear.
Yet Rupert can see the inadequacies of relying on racial
prejudice as an explanation for everything:

> Rupert didn't like the blues. They were carnivals of
> bewilderment for him. The black girls who went there
> were unapproachable. He felt he'd make a fool of him-
> self if he asked a sister to dance and she ignored him
> and turned away. He couldn't comfort himself there —
> as he had done when he'd gone to the Mecca dancing
> halls with his white friends — with the thought that these
> potential partners were demonstrating their innate racism,
> that they wouldn't dance with him because he was black.

Dhondy is good, too, on the tangle of feelings inside white
people who become emotionally involved with blacks:

> "You make yourself out like white trash. Like the
> girls who hang around black clubs looking for a bit of
> black."
> "Don't ever talk to me in that way!" She was
> terrified that there might be some truth in Rupert's
> accusation. She knew that in speech she insisted on
> talking about black people, white people, anybody, as
> though they were the same, knowing that in reality
> there was a world of difference between them. She
> had learnt, especially through Kwate, that she must
> not try to deny or abandon her "whiteness."

The experience of Mary, the white girl in James
Vance Marshall's *Walkabout*, takes her, however, to the
opposite conclusion: that people are people and that
basically there are no differences. Put beside the harsh
truths of Dhondy's world Marshall's thinking seems to be
dangerously sentimental, leading him to a cozy finale that
is at odds with the realities of life. Nevertheless *Walkabout*
has a number of interesting things to say about questions
of color, particularly in analyzing the roots of racial
prejudice. It is twenty years since the book was first
published and it did not appear on a children's list in
America whereas it did in Britain: these are sufficient

comments on the need for more good novels for the young on this and similar themes. It's high time *Walkabout* was re-issued in the United States as a children's book. (The film based on the story departs radically from the author's original intentions; the color issue is almost totally lost.)

The seeds of racial prejudice lie in the fears people have of their way of life — often fought for and jealously guarded — being undermined, and their values being shown up as wanting. It is the same fear that makes Protestants and Catholics in Northern Ireland mistrust each other; that creates the white man's myth of the black man's huge phallus and sexual potency; that makes the heterosexual family man see a gay life-style as a terrible threat; that aids the fascist everywhere, Ku-Klux-Klan or German Nazi. The aboriginal in *Walkabout* can cope; Mary cannot; his ability to help her in a situation in which she would otherwise die she regards not with gratitude but with hostility and suspicion. It shows her up as inadequate; and part of Marshall's success in this book is to give such an attitude credibility:

> Mary looked at the bush boy, and saw in his eyes a gleam of amusement. It angered her, for she knew the cause; Peter's high-pitched, corncraky voice. All the tenets of progressive society and racial superiority combined inside her to form a deep-rooted core of resentment. It was wrong, cruelly wrong, that she and her brother should be forced to run for help to a Negro; and a naked Negro at that.

Marshall is surely right in linking fear of skin color with fear of sex, and focusing, therefore, Mary's hatred of the aboriginal on his nakedness. For her, nudity is synonymous with aberrant sexual behavior; until the black boy is dying, she remains terrified of being assaulted and raped, despite the very obvious evidence that no such thing will at any time occur, for the aboriginal is not in the least bit interested in her sexually: she's a young

• 107

girl; one who, in his society, carries things, helps the male by bearing burdens. Nudity, for him, implies confidence, not only in one's sexuality, but also in one's ability to be in harmony with the natural world, qualities civilized man has lost. Cover it up, Mary feels, and maybe it will all be less of a threat; the power of primitive man — political and social as well as sexual that the black penis symbolizes — will be hidden and the challenge to white supremacy diminished, perhaps even rendered impotent. That would at least be the start of putting the blacks into what she thinks is their proper place; second-class inferior white citizens.

Mildred Taylor, in *Roll of Thunder, Hear My Cry*, comes closer than anyone else to giving us a really good novel about racial prejudice. She is perhaps not so strong on its origins as James Vance Marshall; and, like him, she does not put her story in modern urban terms, opting to set it in the rural American south in the nineteen-thirties. But she is excellent on the *effects* of racial prejudice. She may not analyze in depth the motives behind the actions of her white characters, but their nastiness, their selfishness and greed, their inability to see blacks as human beings, come over vividly to the reader. It's impossible not to feel anger and a sense of burning injustice in reading this book, and the fact that one does so is a measure of the author's success in bringing to life in words both the petty nuisances the blacks have to put up with in her story — shop-keepers serving white people first; black children obtaining copies of school books that are considered no longer fit for white children to use; blacks walking to school while the whites have their own bus — but also the really vile horrors: blacks being hanged for crimes whites would not even be prosecuted for; attacks at night on homes, houses burned down; people maimed and crippled for life.

As literature *Roll of Thunder, Hear My Cry* is undoubtedly superior to *Walkabout*; characterization, narra-

tive skill, command of English, are all of a higher order
than in James Vance Marshall's novel. Its only weakness
is that Mildred Taylor seems uncertain about how much
she can involve the children — Cassie and Stacey Logan,
the central characters — in areas that are the preserve of
the adults: the result is that she is obliged, too often, to
make them eavesdrop at keyholes or through floorboards
on their parents' discussions of what atrocities have recently occurred, and what actions should be taken in reprisal.
In the incidents where the children are directly involved
and the adults are absent, the writing has a freshness and
a directness that is not always so evident in those parts of
the story where they are listeners. Their father's talks
with the lawyer, Mr. Jamison, for instance, or Mama's
plans for boycotting the Wallaces' shop, are not so exciting as Little Man's confrontation with his teacher over
the tattered book, or Stacey's highly successful plan to
get his own back on the odious bus driver by digging a
pot-hole in the road. And the scene where Cassie, as a
result of devious plotting and controlling her anger for
weeks, gives Lillian Jean her come-uppance, has a marvelous feeling of relief and release, of the sweetness of
revenge:

> When I had pinned Lillian Jean securely beneath me, I
> yanked unmercifully on her long, loose hair and de-
> manded an apology for all the names she had called
> me, and for the incident in Strawberry. At first she
> tried to be cute — "Ain't gonna 'pologize to no nigger!"
> she sassed.
> "You wanna be bald, girl?"
> And she apologized. For herself and her father.
> For her brothers and her mother. For Strawberry and
> Mississippi, and by the time I finished jerking at her
> head, I think she would have apologized for the world
> being round had I demanded it.

♦ 109

Cassie and Stacey may not be direct participants in
the worst evils that occur but they are eye-witnesses to

some of them. The spine-tingling fear, the awful insecurity that life in the South — or any place where racial
prejudice is so strong — can produce in the victims is conveyed to the reader in no uncertain terms. There is a very
powerful episode early on in the book when Cassie goes
out in the middle of the night and sees the headlights of
a procession of cars which stop outside her house; shadowy
figures come into the garden, pause, decide that they have
come to the wrong place, then go back to their cars and
drive away— it's the home of some other unfortunate black
family that will be burned down that night:

> I leaned against the latch while waves of sick terror
> swept over me. Realizing that I must get into bed before
> Mama or Big Ma came from the other room, I pulled
> off my muddy clothes, turning them inside out to wipe
> the mud from my body, and put on my night clothes.
> Then I climbed into the softness of the bed. I lay very
> still for a while, not allowing myself to think. But soon,
> against my will, the vision of ghostly headlights soaked
> into my mind and an uncontrollable trembling racked
> my body. And it remained until dawn, when I fell
> into a restless sleep.

Cassie's family, more than most blacks in the area,
are marked out for victimization. They aren't poverty-
stricken illiterate cotton-pickers; they're intelligent, edu-
cated people, owners of four hundred acres of land. Mama
is a teacher, and instrumental in organizing the boycott
of the local shop. They are much more of a threat to
white supremacy than the blacks who accept the status
quo, who mind their own business and bow like reeds
before the storm. A great deal of the tension in the story
is produced by the feeling that the Logans may have over-
reached themselves and become the obvious targets for
the next burning or killing. True, Papa is fired at and
his leg broken as the result of the horse bolting in fright
when it hears the gun-shot, but the family escapes the
worst atrocities one fears may be in store for them. This

does not mean that Mildred Taylor has shirked the issue, feeling, perhaps, that it isn't a suitable subject for a children's book; rather it is a tribute to the skill and cunning one particular family exercises in self-defense and deflecting the attacks on itself. The full weight of racist violence falls on the hapless lad, T. J. Avery, and here the author does perhaps make a concession to the fact that she is writing a children's book rather than a novel for adults. T. J.'s fate — a trial on a murder charge and hanging as the almost inevitable result — would have been exceptionally harrowing for the child reader if it had been made the fate of a member of the Logan family, and Mildred Taylor may well have felt that she did not want to put her audience through such an experience. Perhaps that is an underestimation of what the young can take, but as the book is to a large extent based on real events that happened to the author's father and his family, it would be quite absurd to fault her for telling the truth!

Though T. J. is only fourteen, and the white boys, who are more responsible than he is for Mr. Barnett's death, escape unpunished, the full horror of the tragic waste of a young life is mitigated to some extent by the fact that T. J. is on the whole a thoroughly detestable person; a cheat, a liar, and a thief; the cause of Mrs. Logan losing her job; someone who will side with the whites to the detriment of the blacks when it furthers his own selfish aims. The uneasy friendship between him and Stacey turns to open hostility when T. J. obtains Stacey's winter overcoat under false pretences, and for most of the book the Logan family dislike and disapprove of him, realizing that he is as much of a threat to them as the whites are. The Logans are, of course, as appalled as anyone else by what happens to him, and the ambivalence Cassie feels about this is very well rendered. The last paragraphs of the book show an interesting stage in Cassie's growing up — a discovery that all is not, meta-phorically speaking, black and white, that there are grey areas which are very hard to pinpoint, to sum up, which do demand contradictions of feeling:

> I had never liked T. J., but he had always been there, a part of me, a part of my life, just like the mud and the rain, and I had thought he always would be. Yet the mud and the rain and the dust would all pass. I knew and understood that. What had happened to T. J. in the night I did not understand, but I knew that it would not pass. And I cried for those things which had happened in the night and would not pass.

Mildred Taylor does not, under the surface of her story, convey to the reader the enormously complex issues that are suggested in *Walkabout*, even though she writes a much finer novel, and I doubt if anyone has got down to the roots of the problem, in a children's book, so well as James Vance Marshall has done. The reason, perhaps, is that the issues *are* so complex, so close to us, so relatively new. In England a multi-racial society is an entirely modern phenomenon, and in America the relationships between blacks and whites have in recent years seen radical changes. A stark and simple tale set in the Australian outback may tell us more about the nature of racial prejudice than something with a more obviously contemporary background, simply because when we see the issues on our own doorsteps we don't yet know how to handle them in a story for teenagers or children. I'm not suggesting that all children's books which deal with the problems of color should go back to the Australian desert or the South of the nineteen-thirties for their scenarios; that would be absurd. We certainly need stories for children which discuss the subject in contemporary urban terms, particularly in Britain, and Farrukh Dhondy is one writer who is at least showing the way. But the achievements of James Vance Marshall and Mildred Taylor are not to be ignored.

References

Mildred Taylor
  Roll of Thunder, Hear My Cry Dial 1976; Gollancz 1977

James Vance Marshall
  Walkabout Michael Joseph 1959; Morrow 1959

Farrukh Dhondy
  East End at Your Feet Macmillan, London, 1976
  The Siege of Babylon Macmillan, London, 1978

Paula Fox
  The Slave Dancer Bradbury 1973; Macmillan, London, 1974

Nina Bawden
  On the Run Gollancz 1964; Lippincott 1965 (as *Three on the Run*)
  The Robbers Gollancz 1979; Lothrop 1979

Fay Sampson
  F67 Hamish Hamilton 1975

Naomi Mitchison
  Sunrise Tomorrow Collins, London, 1973

Nat Hentoff
  Jazz Country Harper 1965; Hart-Davis n.d.

"The Colour
of Saying"

♦

PAULA FOX

THE DISTINCTION and beauty of the words she uses
and her absolute command of subtlety and nuance in
rhythms and sentence structure place Paula Fox above
almost all other children's writers. Only Philippa Pearce
can rival her in "the colour of saying," as Dylan Thomas
put it in his poem, "Once it was the colour of saying."
And if *Tom's Midnight Garden* is the outstanding children's book of the fifties and *A Wizard of Earthsea* is
that of the sixties, then *The Slave Dancer* has a good
claim to that title in the seventies. Recognition of her
abilities has not been withheld; she is the recipient of the
Newbery Medal and the Hans Christian Andersen Award,
and her merits have often been acknowledged on both
sides of the Atlantic. So the critic approaches her work
with some awe and some trepidation, hoping that he
will not get bogged down in an excess of superlatives.

Her output, like that of Philippa Pearce, is small.
Most of her writing for children dates from the years
1967-1970 when she produced five brief novels; they are
no longer than novellas or long short stories, and one of
them, *A Likely Place*, is only fifty pages. In the past nine
years she has produced a volume of short stories and one
full-length novel, *The Slave Dancer*. This reluctance to
rush into print may well be wise: she seems to wish to
publish only when she has something worth saying, for
even if the themes of one book are looked at again in
another, the approach is invariably different.

With the exception of *The Slave Dancer*, her novels are concerned with children who suffer from what one would call a deprivation of the imagination — whether they are stories set in derelict urban areas, such as *How Many Miles to Babylon?* or in beautiful houses in wide open rural spaces, as in *The Stone-Faced Boy*. For it isn't environment that usually stultifies in a Paula Fox story, it's adults: not the nasty malevolent figures we find in the work of Paul Zindel, but essentially well-meaning people who just cannot understand how their offspring can want to be different from themselves; who, set as they are in routines of work and house-cleaning and reaching the airport on time, have forgotten that any other way of life has attractiveness or validity. The father in *Portrait of Ivan* is a typical specimen. He expresses a kind of annoyed amazement that his son hasn't taken any photographs when he was on holiday: "What's the point," he says, "of going anywhere if you can't keep a record?" and then he adds, "Someday you may want to see where you've been. Then what will you do?" To which Ivan retorts "But I *know* where I was!" Places, Ivan's father thinks, are to be photographed, labeled, and recorded, not experienced and felt. When Ivan tells his teacher that he is going to Florida for a vacation, her only comment is:

> Florida. Generally low and flat, many swamps, most extensive in south. Oranges, dairy products, cattle, tomatoes, grapefruit, tobacco, snap beans. Textiles, paper, lumber, machinery. July mean temperature, 82.1 degrees Fahrenheit. Land area is 54,252 square miles.

This is strongly reminiscent of the way Bitzer has to define a horse in Dickens's *Hard Times*: Gradgrind and M'Choakumchild still ride high in our schools.

The central characters of her books are often withdrawn, uncommunicative, static people who apparently look at life as if through a glass; stone-faced like Gus, ♦ 115 utterly passive like Ben. (Ben in *Blowfish Live in the Sea* is Gus of *The Stone-Faced Boy* eight years on.) It's significant, for instance, that Gus's first glimpse of his great-aunt is from outside the house; he watches her through a window, and it's interesting that Philippa Pearce, in *A Dog So Small*, took as her central character a similarly introverted boy who is also the third in a family of five children, the odd one out who retreats into a fantasy world inhabited by dogs rather than humans. The states of mind of Paula Fox's children are recorded in terse vivid sentences:

> Eating dinner together had gotten to be like rowing a little boat around inside a live volcano (*Blowfish Live in the Sea*)

> Everyone wanted to help Lewis. That's why he was thinking of running away. (*A Likely Place*)

> Looking at that car, thinking about his life in the city, Ivan realized that he was nearly always being taken to or from some place by an adult, that in nearly every moment of his day he was holding onto a rope held at the other end by a grown-up person... (*Portrait of Ivan*)

> Sometimes he imagined himself as tiny as one of Serena's bugs, running around on the inside of his own head, trying to poke out his mouth so that it would laugh. (*The Stone-Faced Boy*)

And Gus, by being so emotionless in the face of adversity, has a new kind of trouble. "What had happened was that he was no longer shutting that imaginary door. It was shutting itself."

The author doesn't necessarily condone these attitudes. Ben's behavior, for instance, if understandable, is also seen as selfish. " 'Human beings fill up the world with garbage,' he said in his distant I-have-nothing-to-do-with-it voice." And Ivan, seeking self-pitying sympathy, tells Matt and Miss Manderby that his mother died when he was very young — and is somewhat put out when they show no interest. The right kind of adult, Paula Fox seems to be saying, the adult who isn't obsessed with the clock or making money or keeping up a respectable appearance, can help these unfortunate children. There are a number of such people in her books, eccentric oddities, sometimes failures and drop-outs who look at life from a very personal and usually rather strange angle, but who are willing to give children space and time to grow imaginatively and find out who they really are. Great-aunt Hattie, Mr. Felix, Matt, Miss Manderby, Mr. Madruga, Miss Fitchlow . . . the list is long. "There is such a thing in the world as not wanting to do anything special," says Mr. Felix, with characteristic insight, in *Blowfish Live in the Sea*, as he tries to relieve Ben of the conventional pressures. But, ultimately, it is the children themselves who have to make the effort; there is no magic formula, no sure-fire recipe for happiness, that outsiders can give. So Ben decides to stay with his father and not return to his mother; Gus rescues Serena's dog unaided and grows up a little in doing so; Lewis finds that time in school can pass with surprising speed. This realization that they must cope with their own problems is summed up very well on the last page of *The Stone-Faced Boy* when Gus looks at the stone, the geode, which Great-aunt Hattie has given him, and he realizes it's a symbol of himself:

> He knew how the stone would look inside, but he didn't choose to break it open yet. When he felt like it, he would take the hammer and tap the geode in such a way that it would break perfectly, in such a way that not one of the crystals inside would be broken.

Hope, a realization of an inner strength not previously recognized: that is how these books often end.

But what makes the novels of Paula Fox so completely individual is the quality of the writing and the curious way the plots work. At first sight, the story-lines seem thin and aimless, with the exception of *How Many Miles to Babylon?* which has a strong, almost conventional, tale of crooks outwitted — though the story is much less important than the state of mind of the central character, James. Nothing much occurs in *The Stone-Faced Boy*: a dog is lost and found; a great-aunt comes to stay. In *Blowfish Live in the Sea* the only events are a boy and a girl traveling to Boston to see the boy's father; they go out to dinner, and the girl returns to New York. In *A Likely Place* and *Portrait of Ivan* almost nothing at all happens; in the latter book in particular the reader may wonder when he is three-quarters of the way through what the point of it is, and feel bemused about where the author is taking him. Detail follows detail apparently without connection: things seen from a car window, menus, fragments of conversation, descriptions of furniture, anything, one imagines, which happens to be in the author's head at the time. But everything does fall into place eventually; these seemingly disparate bits of jigsaw add up to a complete picture — the portrait of Ivan — and it's only at the end that the reader can look back and see how and why. Miss Manderby, for instance, has no immediately recognizable function in the story; she contributes nothing apart from her conversation, but were she absent the whole experience of the book would be less rich, and one means of helping Ivan to grow would be removed.

How Many Miles to Babylon? is certainly not plotless; it is, Margery Fisher commented in *Growing Point* "something more than a sequence of events." Margot Hentoff said, in *The New York Times Book Review*, that it had "perhaps too dense a plot" — a rather severe judgment, for the story of delinquent children who steal dogs and claim a reward for having "found" them only exists to help James sort out other problems: the absence of his mother, his backwardness at school, having to live in one room with his three kindly but oppressive aunts. It is not a book about *events* of kidnap and rescue so much as an account of the outrage to the victim's feelings, the disorientation, the sensation of the whole known world splitting apart and being rendered meaningless. This

is, of course, a major theme of *The Slave Dancer; How
Many Miles to Babylon?* is almost a pilot run of the idea,
to be worked out in much deeper fashion in the later
book. But *How Many Miles to Babylon?* touches on
things not dealt with elsewhere, the particular kind of
deprivation, for example, that is experienced in overcrowded cities. Aunt Paul shouts, for instance, "I don't
have sleep anymore. Sleep has left me!" Yet this is not
a story of social realism making political points; the black
ghetto is dealt with in so reticent a manner that color is
scarcely commented on. James is a deprived child of any
race anywhere.

It isn't the color of skin that interests Paula Fox so
much as "the colour of saying," the putting down on paper
of ideas in words that again and again seem to the reader
to be individual, beautiful, and memorable. Nowhere is
this more in evidence than in *The Stone-Faced Boy*, where
the evocation of snowbound landscape, like the geode,
perfectly mirrors the state of Gus's mind – frozen, locked
in on itself; in fact, the achievement of fine balance between plot, background, imagery, and character makes
The Stone-Faced Boy the best of these early stories. It
has the quality of an extended prose-poem:

> The sound of the wind was like a great sigh, or a softly
> spoken word he could not quite make out.

(This image is used again, in an entirely different context,
in *The Slave Dancer*, but with equal impressiveness: "How
strange it was to see another ship! A taut sail in the distance
like an unknown word written across the vast expanse of
the sky.")

> All at once he realized the snow had stopped as sudden-
> ly as it had begun. There was no longer the sound of
> the snowflakes, and the wind dropped so that he could
> hear his feet breaking through the crust, making a noise
> like cotton tearing, and he thought of his mother tearing
> up old sheets to make cleaning rags.

♦ 119

> And in the light from a small round window near the
> ceiling he saw dust motes floating. They seemed to give
> off a kind of sound, a kind of low note that midget bees
> might make. That was the sound of the past, and dust
> was its smell.

The child's growing realization of the significance of the
past is a minor, but important, theme of the book, not
only in Gus's developing sensitivity to the house he lives
in "So many people had lived in the Oliver house! It
didn't seem possible. Where had they all gone? What had
become of them?" — but also in a new, if limited, awareness of the past in people, in Great-aunt Hattie and in
the strange elderly couple he meets in the middle of the
night: "She had a light, free laugh and to Gus's surprise
the sound reminded him of Serena. But Serena would
never get so old. How could anyone live so long?"

The power of the past as a thought-provoking and
necessary presence in people's lives also occurs in *Portrait
of Ivan*. The drawing room of the Crowns' mansion is "a
darkened cavern in which massive carved overstuffed
furniture sat in the gloom like monstrous toads"; the house

> looked haunted, but not by ghosts. Ivan felt as if they
> had walked into a private place where things were
> happening that had nothing to do with him and Matt,
> nothing to do with anyone at all. The night air, the
> silver streak of moonlight and the faint sound of water
> lapping the shore seemed to make one simple but un-
> known sound, as though some very large and un-
> imaginable creature were breathing quietly to itself in
> the night.

It makes Ivan think in a way he was unable to think before. He sees Miss Manderby's cat and asks, "Did the cat
see *him* as he saw himself?" — and when he says goodbye
to Geneva he realizes "He had not thought anyone would
ever be sorry to see him go. He had not ever thought
about that at all." An interesting irony that only becomes
apparent when one reads *The Slave Dancer* is the awful

significance of houses like this — old Southern plantation mansions, built on the wealth of a society reliant on slave labor. In *Portrait of Ivan* it is picturesque and harmless:

> The paint was scaling off; there was a yellow tinge to the wood, and a thick twining vine threw its purple-blossomed tendrils across the walls. A broken rocking chair leaned up against a column.

Matt's sole reason for being there is to make drawings of it because it is going to be pulled down; he's only interested because it is "the end of a certain kind of special Southern architecture." But in *The Slave Dancer*:

> The wide porch of the house was empty. Not a leaf moved in the windless air. Then, all at once, a man on a black horse rode into view. He halted. The horse pawed the ground then flung up his head. At that, as though summoned by the horse, three black men ran to the rider and helped him dismount. They dashed before him up the steps to open the door while a fourth man led away the horse.

Suddenly one knows the meaning of what Ivan sensed and couldn't define, the "unknown sound, as though some very large and unimaginable creature were quietly breathing to itself in the night": that almost unimaginable society where people owned human souls. (It's interesting, too, that Philippa Pearce, in *Tom's Midnight Garden* and *The Children of the House*, also gives very different views of the past symbolized in old houses; one as in *Portrait of Ivan*, observed from the present day; the other, as in *The Slave Dancer*, seen as it really was.)

But not all Paula Fox's landscapes are beautiful old mansions and snow-filled fields. She is just as effective evoking the sordid realities of modern city life:

> He was afraid of this street — the old brown houses were all shut up, boards nailed across the doors, windows all broken and nothing to see behind the windows except the dark rooms that always looked like night.
> (*How Many Miles to Babylon?*)

121

> In the bathroom, the toilet gurgled as though it were gargling. It had no seat at all. The sink was about as big as a cereal dish and there were lines of dirt in it like the tidal markings on a wharf. (*Blowfish Live in the Sea*)

Yet the consequences of such surroundings are not all negative. James, in *How Many Miles to Babylon?*, is able to escape from his problems and think of his mother when he plays in a room in an old derelict house — there he can be alone and free from the nagging of his aunts — and Ben finds the squalor of Mr. Felix's hotel less important than finding Mr. Felix himself.

For Jessie, in *The Slave Dancer*, there is no escape. The slave ship is, whatever its size, always a prison; he even clings to his hammock "like a wounded crab clings to a bit of weed." The image of imprisonment is present right from the moment of kidnap — "I was tossed, then trussed, then lifted up and carried like a pig to market" — until the end of the book and beyond; there is no hopeful conclusion here, no release from bondage into the freedoms and choices of adulthood, for what happens to Jessie scars him forever. As a grown man he can say "We were out of the south, but it was not out of me," and for the rest of his life he cannot listen to music, a particularly unpleasant irony when one remembers that it was for his musical ability that he was kidnapped in the first place:

> I would see once again as though they'd never ceased their dancing in my mind, black men and women and children lifting their tormented limbs in time to a reedy martial air, the dust rising from their joyless thumping, the sound of the fife finally drowned beneath the clanging of their chains.

The subject matter of *The Slave Dancer* is vast in scope and implication, making the preoccupations of Paula Fox's previous books seem quite small. It is a savage indictment of a whole society, intensely political in its overtones which ring down through the ages to the present day. After all, James in *How Many Miles to Babylon?* is quite possibly the descendant of a black slave. It's as if Paula Fox were saying to modern America, that is how it was; you're still having to pay for this appalling outrage: this is how it is. Nor can any British reader feel smug and say to himself that it's nothing to do with him; that it's a purely American affair. The parallel drawn in the book, through the character of Purvis, to the English treatment of the Irish, is all too uncomfortably accurate. In England we are still waiting for a novelist who can portray the horrors of 1798, or the Famine, or the Black and Tans, in terms that children can appreciate. It's an astonishing achievement that Paula Fox can use such terrifying, such adult, material as the slave trade and turn out a *children's* book that is something like perfection.

The kidnapped child-narrator obviously helps the child reader, because it immediately places Jessie, in the reader's mind, in the same situation as the hapless blacks; *How Many Miles to Babylon?* also effectively used the idea of a double kidnap, one situation mirroring the other, for not only is James snatched from his surroundings, but so also are the unfortunate dogs. Jill Paton Walsh employed a similar method as an entrance to her material in *The Emperor's Winding Sheet*, although Vrethiki's capture is a less subtle device than Jessie's; it has a reasonably convincing motive, but it isn't central to the story, and Vrethiki is not therefore always the most suitable person to comment on events. Yet Jessie's sufferings never cease to be an oblique comment on the sufferings of the slaves, which we know, as we experience what he feels, are always worse than his. What they have to endure is not dwelt on at length in direct fashion; a few spare details are all that is necessary, and all that are given. If it were done differently, it could not be a novel for children, and what little we are told is in fact almost unbearable:

> I heard groans, the shifting of shackles, the damp sliding
> whisper of sweating arms and legs as the slaves tried

desperately to curl themselves even tighter. I did not
know my eyes were shut until fingers brushed my
cheeks. I saw a man's face not a foot from my own.
I saw every line, every ridge, a small scar next to one
eyebrow, the inflamed lids of his eyes. He was trying
to force his knees closer to his chin, to gather himself up
like a ball on top of the cask upon which he lived. I
saw how ash-colored his knees were, how his swollen
calves narrowed nearly to bone down where the shackles
had cut his ankles, how the metal had cut red trails into
his flesh.

Despite the nature of the subject matter, there is no
unchanging emphasis on pain and horror; there is a quite
remarkable variety of tone throughout the book. Patterns
of emotion shift as the relationships between the characters
develop and alter, as the weather improves or worsens.
Jessie shares jokes and laughter with Purvis; becomes involved in trying to outwit the evil Ben Stout; once, as
he looks at the sea, he feels happy. Attitudes to the slaves
are not consistent; at one moment Jessie even hates them,
seeing them as the sole reason for his being there — why
he's been forcibly uprooted from his home and family.
Then, just as it's impossible for us to understand the nature
of a child-abuser until we see that a child has so exasperated
the abuser that he hits out, so it is impossible for Jessie to
comprehend the feelings of the crew toward the slaves
until, briefly, he himself experiences similar emotions:

> I hated their shuffling, their howling, their very suffer-
> ing! I hated the way they spat out their food on the
> deck, the overflowing buckets, the emptying of which
> tried all my strength. I hated the foul stench that came
> from the holds no matter which way the wind blew,
> as though the ship itself were soaked with human excre-
> ment. I would have snatched the rope from Stout's hand
> and beaten them myself! Oh, God! I wished them all
> dead! Not to hear them! Not to smell them! Not to
> know of their existence!

This is ironically contrasted with a brief change in some

of the sailors, who, in a good mood because the voyage is for the moment working out well, play with the slave children, giving them "extra water from their own slim rations and fashioning rough toys of wood to amuse them." But usually the men are pitiless; at best they "were silent, and avoided the holds as much as they could."

Ironies abound in this novel. It is an escaped slave who, in the end, saves Jessie's life after the ship is wrecked. The blacks, despite their predicament, have a dignity that rarely falters, and that makes the behavior of the captain and the mate seem worse than the instincts of the most savage animals. Jessie feels the nakedness of the slaves adds to their helplessness — "even if we had not been armed, our clothes and boots alone would have given us power" — though no amount of clothes and boots and arms can in the end save the crew from drowning when the ship is destroyed in a storm. The book consists of layers of meaning, of nuance within nuance, and only several readings can bring out the full richness of it.

And on its surface, like the ship on the surface of the sea, the prose, as in all of Paula Fox's work, dazzles and delights with its poetry:

> For some time after the sun had set, the sky remained the color of rope. The ship lay steady on the glass-like surface of the water which was pricked, now and then, into small ripples when a sea-bird struck its surface. There was a smoky indistinct look to the Cuban shore. The birds disappeared, their last cries lingering in my ears the way strands of light cling briefly to the masts after the sun has vanished.

Or Jessie's amazement when he is informed that the ship is bound for Africa: "for all the calmness with which he said *Africa*, he might as well have said Royal Street. I felt like a bird caught in a room." This is as powerful in its terseness, its sense of being dumb-struck, as the moment when Esther Rudomin, in *The Endless Steppe*, is told something very similar: that she's in Siberia. There is a masterly use on every page of rhythm and cadence; the very essence of the way the sea shifts and slides, for example, is expressed in one sentence: "I heard from far off the great breathing of the sea, taken in, expelled."

One of the reasons for Paula Fox's pre-eminence is that she never underestimates the child's ability to absorb implication, suggestion, and analogy. Her material, with the exception of *The Slave Dancer*, is not unlike the territory of many contemporary American authors: children seeking a lost parent; children who are imaginatively and emotionally starved. But the way she constructs her plots and the way she uses the English language make her second to none. And in *The Slave Dancer* she has given us a masterpiece, the equal of which would be hard to find.

References

PAULA FOX

A Likely Place Macmillan, New York, 1967; Macmillan, London, 1968
How Many Miles to Babylon? David White 1967; Macmillan, London, 1968
The Stone-Faced Boy Bradbury 1968; Macmillan, London, 1969
Portrait of Ivan Bradbury 1969; Macmillan, London, 1970
Blowfish Live in the Sea Bradbury 1970; Macmillan, London, 1972
The Slave Dancer Bradbury 1973; Macmillan, London, 1974

PHILIPPA PEARCE

Tom's Midnight Garden Oxford, 1958; Lippincott 1959
A Dog So Small Constable 1962; Lippincott 1963

BRIAN FAIRFAX-LUCY AND PHILIPPA PEARCE

The Children of the House Longman 1968; Lippincott 1968

URSULA K. LE GUIN

A Wizard of Earthsea Parnassus 1968; Gollancz 1971

CHARLES DICKENS
    Hard Times first published in 1854

JILL PATON WALSH
    The Emperor's Winding Sheet Macmillan, London,
    1974; Farrar 1974

ESTHER HAUTZIG
    The Endless Steppe Crowell 1968; Hamish Hamilton
    1969

MARGERY FISHER
    review in *Growing Point* of *How Many Miles to
    Babylon?*

MARGOT HENTOFF
    review in *New York Times Book Review* of *How
    Many Miles to Babylon?*

Making the
Children Stretch

◆

NINA BAWDEN

NINA BAWDEN established herself as an author for adults before she started to write juvenile fiction, and her first six books for young people seem to reflect an implicit belief that the novel for children is a totally different genre from the novel for adults — that what may interest the child reader is likely to be quite different from what is of concern to the mature person. From *The Secret Passage* to *The Runaway Summer*, written and published in the 1960s, adults play only a peripheral part in the action, but with her books published in the 1970s, from *Squib* to *The Robbers*, the opposite is true: Adults are central to the stories, and instead of creating a world in which the grown-ups are more or less excluded so that the children can happily solve all the problems, Nina Bawden is concerned to show, particularly in *Carrie's War* and *The Peppermint Pig*, how the lives of the old and the young are, for better or worse, inextricably bound together.

The books up to and including *The Runaway Summer* are generally inferior in quality to those that follow, and the reader who marvels at the astonishing richness and originality of *The Peppermint Pig* may well feel disappointed by the thinness of some of its predecessors. These early novels use many of the clichés of plot that can be found in most second-rate escapist books for the young: the child protagonists camp out on an idyllic island in an endless hot summer, or catch thieves before

the police arrive, outwit kidnappers, discover a secret
passage, are rewarded by inheriting a fortune or being
offered a holiday abroad, or they find out that the nasty
grown-ups love them after all: everyone lives happily
ever after. It is much the same material as one might find
in Enid Blyton. Improbability looms large on every page.
Simon in *The Runaway Summer* is allowed to stay away
from home for weeks without his parents even asking
where he is; Ben in *On the Run* climbs with great ease
an extremely dangerous cliff in the dark in a raging storm;
an escaped wolf appears at the climax of *The White Horse
Gang* just to add a little spice to an already complicated
and tense situation. Penelope Lively, in "Children and
Memory," defined fantasy, in the worst sense of the word,
as the kind of tale in which "people arc either children —
and therefore heroic and at the centre of things — or adult
— and therefore evil or else conveniently negative." These
early stories of Nina Bawden's appear to belong to this
category — escapist light-weight stuff, forgotten as soon
as read. They certainly aren't in the least like real life,
even though they may pretend to be.

Children, just like adults, need escapist literature of
course; and, in any case, it is perhaps too severe a judgment to dismiss these novels completely. There are areas
of interest other than the excitement of a fast-moving plot.
Characterization is sometimes very good — the gang of
kids in *A Handful of Thieves* are sharply individualized;
Ben Mallory, the hero of both *The Secret Passage* and
On the Run comes over as a strong, resourceful, and attractive person; Abel in *The White Horse Gang* is a well-
observed delineation of a canny peasant child. The weakest
book in this respect is *The Witch's Daughter* — no one
seems to come alive as a fully-developed, real person —
and it is feeble, too, in not giving the reader any sense of
being set in a real place. The distant Scottish island on
which the action occurs remains a figment of the author's
imagination rather than a genuinely dramatic and beautiful

piece of harsh landscape; whereas Henstable, the seaside town in the south of England which forms the background to *The Secret Passage*, *The Runaway Summer* and much of *On the Run*, is created with an eye for telling detail — a decayed genteel resort, full of dogs, frail old people and humorless landladies; a cold place, respectable and dull.

There is the occasional perception or image which remains in the memory. The windows of a house in *The White Horse Gang* "looked like dead eyes"; Henstable in *The Secret Passage* is full of houses that "all seemed very tall and narrow and somehow sloping, as if the fierce, cold wind from the sea had blown them sideways." And, under the surface, serious themes are mentioned, considerations that are not normally found in escapist literature. There is a concern for the old, an awareness that society often gives them a raw deal. Gran, in *A Handful of Thieves*, says

> Once you get old, you can't be too careful. You're no help to anyone and a nuisance to most — it's best to toe the line and be no more of a nuisance than you can help.

She suggests that it is much the same for children, a feeling echoed by Mary in *The Runaway Summer*:

> Mary thought that old people were often no better off than children, with other grown-ups always bullying them and knowing what was best for them and making them wear vests and drink cocoa.

The problems of a multi-racial society are touched on — though never fully discussed — in *The Secret Passage*, *On The Run*, and *The Runaway Summer*. Ben, whose earliest years were spent in Africa, and whose best friend was a black, is shocked by racist attitudes in England, and in *The Runaway Summer* Nina Bawden makes her own views about the unfairness of British immigration laws quite clear — going so far as to suggest, in the person of

Aunt Alice, that "some laws are made to be broken." But it is disappointing to find that the black characters, Krishna in *The Runaway Summer* and Tom in *On the Run*, are not properly developed, as if the author felt she did not quite know how to deal with them in a children's novel. Occasionally, however, there are some nice humorous moments: Aunt Mabel's preconceived ideas in *On the Run*, for instance, are seen not as evil but as harmless and amusing:

> She looked at her brother-in-law. "He's a fine man, Chief Okapi. Sat at the table and ate his chicken just like anyone else."
>
> "What did you expect, Mabel?" Mr. Mallory asked curiously.
>
> "I really don't know," she said in a surprised voice and stuck her long, pink nose in the air.

The most effective of these early novels is *The White Horse Gang*. The plot — which deals with the attempts of a group of kids to kidnap and hold for ransom the unpopular "mother's boy," Percy, the son of wealthy parents — is neither original nor particularly credible, but the story takes on a nice twist when Percy refuses to take the kidnap seriously: to him it is a splendid game, a release from his oppressive, nagging mother. At last he's free, allowed to ride a horse, to get his hands and face dirty without anyone telling him off; he can enjoy all sorts of physical exercise in the open air. When Sam and Abel decide to abandon the kidnap attempt because it is too dangerous and likely to land them in serious trouble, they have an almost impossible task trying to persuade Percy to go home. The pace of this book is more leisurely than the others; everything, for once, is not subordinated to the demands of the plot. The author has time to describe a number of small incidents that illustrate character rather than push the narrative ahead; she can afford to pause and describe scenery and background, give the reader a proper sense of place. So a small rural community in

♦ 131

Shropshire is made to come alive, and the characters are given a life that seems larger than merely responding to events. Sam's battles with his teacher, Miss Pennyfather, are an amusing side-issue. Finding a dead rat in her desk gives Miss Pennyfather no qualms:

> She merely used it as an excuse to give them an extremely long Nature Study lesson on the habits of the rat, including a graphic description of various rat-borne diseases like bubonic plague, which put Rose — and most of the girls in the class — off their dinner.

Yet when Sam replaces, in the dead of night, the Christmas tree he has given her with a much larger specimen (she has been overemphasizing in her nature lessons the fact that trees and plants *grow*) she is hurt and baffled, and this makes him far more miserable and penitent than any scolding or punishment would have done.*

With the exception of *The White Horse Gang*, one feels that Nina Bawden is not stretching herself in these books. They are all exercises in various kinds of plot which she can handle easily and which she knows are popular and make few demands on her readers. The publication in 1971 of *Squib*, however, shows a radical change of direction. In this novel and its successors — particularly *Carrie's War* and *The Peppermint Pig* — the conventional story-lines are abandoned in favor of a looser framework in which narrative excitement becomes less important, and the relationships between children and adults are increasingly significant. Nina Bawden, in *Squib*, is not only stretching herself but also her readers, and

---

*These two incidents do not occur in the American edition of *The White Horse Gang*. The American publisher felt that the fourth chapter of the book was too long, and insisted on making some cuts. This kind of editing, which used to be fairly common in American editions of British children's books — and in British editions of American books — is, fortunately, not practised so frequently nowadays, though it still occurs. The American edition of one of my own novels, *Quintin's Man*, is a mutilated travesty of the original.

the demands grow with almost every succeeding book.

Squib is a strange child, match-stick thin, dressed in old-fashioned clothes. Sometimes his legs are covered with painful bruises. For Kate, a dreamy, neurotic girl whose father and brother were drowned some years previously, Squib seems to be a ghost; he has the same eyes as her dead brother — one blue, and one brown. For Prue and Sammy, the cleaning lady's children, he's the victim of an ogre who keeps him locked up in a castle: Squib seems to live in a huge Victorian mansion (which is, in fact, an old people's home) and he can occasionally be observed, looking wistfully out of its top-floor windows. For practical, sensible Robin — Prue's and Sammy's older brother — he's an object of no interest at all, until it becomes obvious that Squib isn't a figment of Kate's and Prue's and Sammy's imagination, but a real person who is being brutally maltreated by his stepmother. The climax of the book is melodramatic, with the drowning idea being unnecessarily repeated when Kate and Squib are saved from death by Robin's mother, and the ending is a bit too much like a fairy-tale (Squib is adopted by Robin's sister.) But the sequences that lead to the climax are most effective, and though it is a short book, the characters are firmly established. The changing patterns of the relationships between the children as they become more involved with Squib are extremely convincing, and particularly well done is the uneasy early adolescent friendship between Kate and Robin. The main theme of the book — that nothing is quite what it seems to be, that we each interpret events according to our own needs and desires — is admirably illustrated in the behavior and reactions of all the characters. In *Squib*, children are exposed to the corruption and selfishness of certain aspects of adult life. Kate and Robin learn a great deal when they witness the appalling conduct of Squib's step-parents to each other, and the squalor of their feckless existence at a trailer park:

He stepped over Robin, climbed the steps of the bus, and looked in. Silence for a moment, stillness and silence, and then he said, "God damn this rotten life."

Kate thought these were the saddest words she ever heard... She felt as if something were bleeding inside her. He slumped off, shambling and heavy like a tired, old bear, and she watched him out of sight.

Carrie's War is about children under stress in wartime. Carrie and her younger brother, Nick, are evacuated to a remote town in North Wales, and the feelings of bewilderment and disorientation that must have afflicted many British children in 1939, uprooted from family and home and dispatched to distant parts of the country where they were often made to feel very unwelcome, are vividly realized. But worse than this is to follow for Carrie and Nick. They find themselves staying with Samuel Evans, a bad-tempered, pompous, bullying, elderly grocer with no understanding of children, and his pathetic, ineffectual sister, Louise. Against their will the children are caught up in events over which they have little control — a battle of wits between Mr. Evans and his elder sister, Dilys Gotobed. Dilys married a rich Englishman and thus mortally offended her brother; the question is, now that she is old and dying, who is to inherit her property? Carrie is used as a pawn, a spy, a go-between taking messages. She comes through her ordeal unscathed, but the insight she obtains into the weaknesses of certain adults jolts her sharply into growing up. And it jolts the reader too. Nina Bawden has no hesitation in this book in pointing out to the child reader that adults do not necessarily offer security and love to the young; they may merely be interested in exploiting them for their own selfish ends.

Mr. Evans is perhaps the most vivid and well-drawn character Nina Bawden has ever created; particularly memorable is the picture of him at the conclusion of the book, a broken man, old and alone. He has lost everything — both his sisters and the property he coveted — and he no longer seems to be a monster of egotism; he is only a foolish, selfish soul whose plans have all been thwarted. Solitude is his punishment. It is one of the triumphs of the novel that the reader feels sorry for him. Less successful, perhaps, is the portrayal of Dilys Gotobed, half-crazed and self-dramatizing, and her mysterious witch-like housekeeper, Hepzibah Green. They do not belong to the harsh, bleak, real world of most of the story but to another genre: that of the gothic, romantic scenario, typified by Daphne du Maurier's *Rebecca*. The two conventions do not marry easily. But it is a minor fault. Above all, this is a book about evacuation, displacement, the fortunes of war; and the war in the Evans family is given a rich background metaphor in the public events of 1939-1945, far away perhaps, but nevertheless happening at the same time. All in all, *Carrie's War* seems a much more truthful account of the pressures on children at that date than, for example, Robert Westall's *The Machine Gunners*, with its emphasis on spurious male virtues like "guts" and the necessity to hit your opponent as hard as possible. Nina Bawden stresses integrity rather than guts, and shows us the much more interesting and credible violence that exists *inside* the human personality, in children as well as adults, and the variety of ways different people employ, either to suppress or to come to terms with such feelings, or to cajole others into courses of action that are contrary to what they naturally want to follow. The conflict within is well summed up by remarks like "A great wind of rage seemed to blow her along the passage, flung the door open and then dropped her, becalmed, just inside it." The reader is asked to examine problems from every possible point of view. There is, the author seems to be saying, no absolute right or wrong.

The Peppermint Pig, however, is undoubtedly her finest book so far. Set at the turn of the century in a small country town, its story deals with a year in the lives of the Greengrass family — the year in which Father is away in America, and in which Poll, the youngest child, endures a great deal of painful growing up. It is quite different from any of Nina Bawden's other novels in a number of respects. There is no firm story-line at all; instead we are given a series of self-contained incidents — Poll suffering from scarlet fever; Theo's battles with the unpleasant Noah Bugg; Poll's revenge on Lady March's nasty servants; and so on — yet the story has a remarkable sense of unity, largely brought about by the superb evocation of provincial life in Edwardian times, the rhythms of the seasons, the lush, flat, East Anglian landscape:

> The noises continued: a delicate squealing and chirping; a hushed sighing like a calm sea washing pebbles; a rustling and scattering; a low mysterious whistle; a sweet, musical bleating...
> "Sheep going by," Mother said. She wrapped Poll in a blanket and carried her to the window. Day was a pale lemon streak over the rooftops; below, in the Square, the flock and the shepherds passed in blue shadow, iron hurdle wheels squeaking, dainty hooves pattering, baby lambs baa-ing, the dog at their heels giving low-pitched little yelps as if he did not want to disturb the slumbering town.

Nina Bawden in this novel is writing about her ancestors who came from Swaffham, Norfolk; a hundred little details and remembered anecdotes, handed down from generation to generation, are lovingly recorded: the total effect is like a superbly patterned mosaic. All the characters come vividly alive, from the most important — the complex and admirable Emily Greengrass, who, in middle age, still has an immense capacity for fun despite the family's financial troubles:

> She put the hunting horn to her lips, and, standing in the middle of the wide Market Square, blew a long wailing blast that echoed back from the houses and silenced them all

— to the merely peripheral, Marigold Bugg, for instance, who

> seemed to sway rather than walk, with a boneless wavy motion that made Poll think of a caterpillar.

The pleasures and vicissitudes of living in a large close-knit family that has come down in the world are strongly emphasized. One striking image at the end of the books points to Nina Bawden's purpose; Poll hears her parents, her sister, and her brothers all talking at once: their voices are "all running into and over each other like instruments in an orchestra." The musical analogy is illuminating; ideas, characters, and descriptions occur, recur, are developed, dropped, taken up later, giving a total effect of immense richness; what one reads on the page, one feels, is as densely packed as a movement in a symphony. The Greengrass family also live *between* the pages of the book, and before it begins and after it ends. The lack of a coherent story, and the now familiar theme of children being caught in and influenced by the problems and actions of the adults who are closest to them, as in *Squib* and *Carrie's War*, make the young reader stretch up to the author rather than suggesting that the author is coming down to the child's level.

Nina Bawden's most recent books are *Devil by the Sea*, *Rebel on a Rock*, and *The Robbers*. None of them achieves the perfection of *The Peppermint Pig*, yet they are all interesting. *Devil by the Sea* is probably the only young adult novel ever to be published which deals with paedophilia. The rape and murder of a young girl is a subject that will produce violent and emotive reactions in everyone; it shows, therefore, considerable courage to write about it in a story for what the author calls "older children." *Devil by the Sea* is, in fact, a recasting of a book that was originally published on an adult list twenty years ago: it is an interesting reflection on the changing attitudes toward children's fiction that it is now thought to be suitable material for the young reader. And of course it *is* suitable: the sexual interest of certain people in pre-pubescent children is something the young should be aware of and warned about. Again, the older characters in this novel are central to the action; the shaky marriage of Alice and Charles Bray is analyzed in some detail, and the young reader is once more permitted to glimpse the complex world of adult problems.

Rebel on a Rock and *The Robbers* are both attempts to combine certain elements of Nina Bawden's earlier books — the exciting adventure story involving children — with moments of crisis in the lives of adults. Neither succeeds totally. In *Rebel on a Rock*, a family on holiday abroad is unwillingly caught up in the political dramas of the country they are visiting (exactly which country is not specified, but it's presumably Greece, at the end of the colonels' regime), and though the narrative is strong and the characters convincing, the novel is weak in its sense of place: the author's talents which recreated Edwardian Norfolk so well do not extend, alas, to describing, memorably, aspects of life in modern Greece. *The Robbers* is concerned with a "tug of love" case. Who should have custody of Philip — his father or his grandmother? There is a lot of selfishness and bad feeling, but Philip's wishes are taken into account at the end. Someone, of course, inevitably gets hurt — in this case, Philip's stepmother. Again, it is a subject once thought to be a totally adult preserve, but it is obviously proper material for a children's book, as it deals with a problem in which children are the central concern. The story, however, is weak in its portrayal of working-class characters: the black woman, Addie, is made to be quite impossibly good and heroic, and her white brother-in-law, Darcy, a supposedly rough Cockney kid, turns out to be far too angelic to be credible. Addie is, in fact, particularly bothersome; for the increasing demands of various pressure groups make it difficult nowadays for a white author to portray black

138 ◆

characters who have even the least trace of wickedness —
"racist" is the immediate reaction — and Addie seems to be
a sop to these quite unjustifiable and extremely irritating
demands.

The Secret Passage was published in 1963, *The
Robbers* in 1979. During that period of time Nina Bawden
has developed and changed enormously as a writer. Those
sixteen years show an interesting shift in fashions and tastes
in children's fiction, and also a great opening-up of areas
previously thought to be outside the range of books for
the young. One of Nina Bawden's greatest strengths has
been her ability to move into these new areas, taking the
children with her, demanding a deeper and more complex
response, but never once offering something the child
cannot grasp. It is well summed up by the author's
comment on Hilary's state of mind at the end of *Devil by
the Sea*:

> She was absorbed in a world of new discoveries: that
> other people are not to be relied upon; that promises
> can be broken; loyalty abandoned; the world that is
> also childhood's end.

References

NINA BAWDEN

The Secret Passage Gollancz 1963; Lippincott 1964
(as *The House of Secrets*)
On the Run Gollancz 1964; Lippincott 1965
(as *Three on the Run*)
The White Horse Gang Gollancz 1966; Lippincott 1966
The Witch's Daughter Gollancz 1966; Lippincott 1966
A Handful of Thieves Gollancz 1967; Lippincott 1967
The Runaway Summer Gollancz 1969; Lippincott 1969
Squib Gollancz 1971; Lippincott 1971
Carrie's War Gollancz 1973; Lippincott 1973
The Peppermint Pig Gollancz 1975; Lippincott 1975
Devil by the Sea Gollancz 1976; Lippincott 1976

◆ 139

    Rebel on a Rock Gollancz 1978
    The Robbers Gollancz 1979; Lothrop 1979

PENELOPE LIVELY
    "Children and Memory" in *The Horn Book Magazine*,
    August 1973

DAPHNE DU MAURIER
    Rebecca Gollancz 1939; Doubleday 1948

ROBERT WESTALL
    The Machine Gunners Macmillan, London, 1975;
    Greenwillow 1976

Types of Ambiguity

◆

JILL PATON WALSH

THE NOVELS of Jill Paton Walsh are invariably well received by adults, and they are popular with children in both America and Great Britain. Assessment of her work comes near to the uncritical adulation that surrounds Alan Garner, and this does her reputation a disservice; it tends to mask her faults and does not determine precisely enough what her particular virtues are. She does not have, in my opinion, "a most perceptive understanding of the unspoken emotions of early adolescence," as *The Daily Telegraph* reviewer said of *Goldengrove*; yet as a historical novelist she has many qualities that make her a worthy inheritor of a long tradition of writers for children — of whom Rosemary Sutcliff is perhaps the greatest living exponent. There are also defects of style that seem to pass unnoticed, among them a clumsiness or uncertainty about what kind of "voice" to adopt: Put any page of *Goldengrove* beside any page of *Tom's Midnight Garden* or *The Stone-Faced Boy* and the reader is made quickly aware of an author struggling to express herself as opposed to one who has total mastery of language. Furthermore, her books raise interesting and awkward questions about what one can only call the "politics" of historical novels for children.

Hengest's Tale has a complicated plot revolving round violent family feuds, bloodshed and revenge, and it is set in the Dark Ages. It seems at first sight to be rather unpromising material for a writer making her debut, but out of such apparently intractable stuff Jill Paton Walsh

◆ 141

makes a rattling good story, the particular strengths of which are a very deft handling of narrative and a pleasing ambiguity in the characterization: it is without goodies or baddies, and events happen because people behave through a mixture of motives; selfishness and generosity are of equal measure in all the protagonists. The reader becomes involved and cares about what occurs, which isn't always easy with characters who speak in a kind of language far removed from our own speech (and probably their own):

> "Son of Witta," said Folcwald, "it is not likely that I shall regret honour done to a man such as you, whose fame for wisdom and good counsel has spread far and wide. You are welcome here with all those you bring. Tomorrow I shall summon my advisers, and before them you shall unlock your word-hoard for all to hear."

In fact there is remarkably little dialogue, and this may have been a wise decision, simply because we have no idea how people actually spoke in the Dark Ages, and it's difficult to invent a convincing language for them; this is a problem that plagues the historical novelist.

The virtues of *Hengest's Tale* — a strong narrative and complex characters — are curiously absent from Jill Paton Walsh's two Second World War novels, *The Dolphin Crossing* and *Fireweed*, and in fact, they do not reappear until *The Emperor's Winding Sheet*. This is probably because the background material is allowed to impose too much of its own shape on the story; in *The Dolphin Crossing* nothing much happens until the two boys arrive at Dunkirk, and in *Fireweed* the London blitz becomes the central event rather than the developing relationship between Bill and Julie. The characters, particularly in *The Dolphin Crossing*, are two-dimensional, maybe because the author's — and our own — attitudes to this period of history are also two-dimensional: There are no ambiguities about Dunkirk or the bombing of London; we know who was right and who was wrong. There's no space for grey areas; it's all black and white. So the old-fashioned virtues of heroism, endurance, dignity in defeat, and their corresponding opposite vices are laid out for our inspection. "Manly" and "noble" are adjectives the author frequently summons to her aid. Cowardice is not examined here as a facet of the human personality needing our sympathy and understanding; it's dismissed as intolerable. Andrew, the conscientious objector in *The Dolphin Crossing*, would have made a more interesting central character than either John or Pat, but, rather maddeningly, he's left on the edges of the plot. The view of life presented by these two novels seems to me to be dangerously and untenably simplistic. It shows not so much how the British really were at that time as how they liked — and still like — to be seen, particularly by others in time of war; it's the "official" line. A book for children set in the nineteen-forties doesn't have to be like this; Robert Westall's *The Machine Gunners*, Nina Bawden's *Carrie's War*, or Penelope Lively's *Going Back* are not. But part of the reason for the success of *Fireweed* and *The Dolphin Crossing* lies in the fact that when they were published there were remarkably few books available about *children* during the Second World War, particularly children in Britain. Since then there has been a spate of them, probably because, as David James said in "Recent World-War-II Fiction," "writing maturity has only recently been attained by many authors who were children then, whose formative years were spent scattered over sundry pastoral retreats of the British Isles, awaiting news from home, or cramped into shelters hoping only for survival." Jill Paton Walsh, in *The Dolphin Crossing* and *Fireweed*, had the luck — or good sense — to be first in this particular field.

There is also an ineptitude in her handling of working class characters. Pat, in *The Dolphin Crossing*, doesn't really speak like a Londoner; his words are closer to the stage Cockney of old British films, exemplifying middle

♦ 143

class assumptions about how such people talk, rather than the genuine article. The problem is worse in *Fireweed* because it's a first-person narration; Bill is a working class boy at a grammar school, and Jill Paton Walsh struggles, unsuccessfully, throughout the whole book to make him sound right. All too often he speaks with two voices, his own — a not properly realized jaunty slang — and the author's:

> Half the great east window of the hall had been blown out, and was lying across the pavement around the foot of Richard Coeur de Lion, and his bronze horse. I remembered how black the yawning gap in the tracery looked. It brought things home to me, that. Seeing ugly old shops and shabby houses knocked apart had not seemed as appalling as seeing the wreckage of that lovely patterned stone.

"It brought things home to me, that" is Bill; "great east window," "yawning gap in the tracery," "the wreckage of that lovely patterned stone" is someone older, the intellectual appreciating points of good architecture: in other words, Jill Paton Walsh. And Bill would have said Richard the Lionheart, not Coeur de Lion. The confusion is added to by some rather romantic-magazine-prose — "I saw her face, a frozen mask, with pools of black fear for eyes, framed in her dark hair, crossed by long wind-blown strands" — and leaden sentences like "I flung back my head, and howled, like a dog, at the sky" which does not adequately convey the idea of a boy in tears.

But the chief defect of *Fireweed* is the failure to make the relationship between Bill and Julie particularly interesting. Julie is prim and a bit insipid, but no matter; it's the shying away from the emotional and sexual implications of adolescent love that is bothersome, especially when the characters are pushed by events into living together and taking under their wing a younger child to whom they become surrogate parents. One doesn't ask for the approach of a Judy Blume, but the reader does need some portrayal of the characters' feelings, however muted, because otherwise Bill and Julie are little more than a device on which to peg the author's primary concerns — the descriptions of the blitz — which on their own would not make a successful story.

These descriptions are, in fact, excellent. They reveal Jill Paton Walsh's real power as a writer, as do the Dunkirk scenes in *The Dolphin Crossing*: a gift for rendering in words some of the big moments of history, vividly bringing to the mind's eye the heat of battle in all its chaos, glory, and horror. The quality of the prose rises to an altogether finer level, and the handling of detail never obscures the general outlines. She is, for once, completely at ease and in command of what she is trying to do. One also admires the lack of sentimentality in Pat's death at the end of *The Dolphin Crossing*: a much more likely event than the soft option of allowing both boys to return unscathed. These scenes remind one of the great historical painters; a picture by Géricault in words. Too little attention has been paid to her achievements in this area. Nobody, not even Rosemary Sutcliff, can do a siege or a naval engagement or a crowded battlefield as well as Jill Paton Walsh, and it is this particular ability that makes *The Emperor's Winding Sheet* one of the most interesting of modern historical novels for children.

However, before she turned to the daunting complexities of the fall of Constantinople to the Turks in 1453, she wrote *Goldengrove*, a very different kind of book. The story, which is an even thinner narrative than either *The Dolphin Crossing* or *Fireweed*, is about the friendship between two teenage cousins, Madge and Paul, who are on holiday at their grandmother's house in Cornwall. They are hovering on the brink of falling in love, until it's revealed that they are not cousins but brother and sister: a somewhat melodramatic and unlikely state of affairs. It seems highly improbable that Madge would have no idea, not even a tiny hint, that Paul was her brother, nor are the reasons she has not been told before strong enough to suggest credibility. Much the most interesting part of the novel is the relationship between Madge and one of her grandmother's tenants, a blind university professor. The description of blindness, the attendant problems of such a major disability, and Madge's reactions, are all convincing; at this stage of the book the reader is fully engaged with what is going on, but, unfortunately, it remains undeveloped, not central to the plot, nor does it make an adequate comment or parallel to the main thread of the narrative.

Goldengrove shows a complete change in Jill Paton Walsh's manner of writing, almost as if she was dissatisfied with her previous style. It's written in the present tense (an awkward unsettling device from the reader's point of view), in a sort of *pointilliste* prose that reminds one of Virginia Woolf; and comparison with Virginia Woolf becomes unavoidable when one realizes that the setting of the novel – St. Ives – is the same as that used in *To the Lighthouse*. Even the houses in the two books are similar – large dignified buildings with terraces outside, rose gardens, dramatic views of the sea, lighthouse and all – redolent of a way of life that vanished with the First World War. But what in Virginia Woolf's novel is a very powerful instrument for portraying the surface of existence, past and present, and everything that lies under that surface, is in Jill Paton Walsh's book an unashamed nostalgia, an invitation to escape; the result is self-indulgent and unsatisfying. Even to Madge at fifteen, Goldengrove and its methods of doing things – leisurely, upper middle class, insulated – are preferable to "real" life, and the reader is asked to share this attitude. Such an invitation is, again, dangerous and simplistic. The writing also seems undisciplined; it is over-descriptive and repetitive, far too adjectival, and even if at times the author manages to pinpoint Madge's feelings effectively, she rarely succeeds in telling the reader how things actually look, nor does she, for example, in all the endless descriptions of the sea, convey its rhythms, sounds, and movements as tellingly as does Paula Fox in that memorable sentence in *The Slave Dancer*, "I heard from far off the great breathing of the sea, taken in, expelled."

Yet Jill Paton Walsh's weakest book was followed by her best, *The Emperor's Winding Sheet*. The characters, for once, have a life that appears to extend outside the confines of the novel; one is led to think of them in situations before the story begins and after it ends. Where one is not tempted, after reading *The Dolphin Crossing*, to do some research on Dunkirk, — not because we know more of the events of 1940 than those of 1453, but because the author doesn't make us want to — the historical background of *The Emperor's Winding Sheet* is so fascinating and so well done that the reader wants to go at once to the source material and discover more about the final years of the Byzantine Empire and its last ruler, Constantine XI. And here, too, is that interesting ambiguity one noticed in *Hengest's Tale*: the Christians aren't all good heroic characters united in a common cause; there is greed, dissension, treachery, and, more interestingly, indecision and inefficiency — a mixture of motives. It is stressed that the Turkish victory — a Tolstoyan view, this — was decided, like so many events that altered the course of history, not by great deeds or by inevitable processes beyond the control of the protagonists, but by mere chance; in this case, the carelessness of the Genoese mercenaries in forgetting to shut a small door. Convincing, too, is the portrayal of the shabbiness of the last years of Constantinople; the churches falling to rack and ruin because nobody had any money to repair them; the painted glass dishes masquerading as gold plate; the whole thin facade of a toy empire living on a shoestring budget and its memories of long-dead splendor. Here are the final   ♦ 147
moments of a thousand years of tradition, of unparalleled power, influence and artistic achievement, collapsing —

beautifully symbolized by the bag of dust the Emperor always carries with him. So here are parallels with our times; our problems and preoccupations are in fact closer to the ambiguities and difficulties of Constantine than to those of John and Pat hauling the exhausted soldiers off the Dunkirk beaches.

Jill Paton Walsh's handling of the big events, the Emperor's coronation, the last Mass in Santa Sophia, the siege itself, is magnificent. Maybe there are bits of stilted dialogue of the "How has it gone today, Sire?" type and Manuel's comment "Never say die" is a jarring piece of twentieth century slang; but they are few, lost in the mastery the author has of her subject matter and her characters. The evocation of weather and scenery is much better done than in *Goldengrove*; a bit lush perhaps, but in this context, effective:

> Lilac against a rose-pink sky lay the long promontory of the City, hovering dreamlike above the silver sea. It was much nearer now: a lovely complex shape, topped with slender columns, laden with swelling domes. As they drew nearer, and day vanished, Vrethiki half expected the vision to fade and vanish, so unearthly and insubstantial did it seem, but it solidified, and took on shape and detail in the gentle morning light.

The author's vision and Vrethiki's are one and the same, unlike those in *Fireweed* and *Goldengrove*, where what Bill and Madge see is obscured by the intrusion of Jill Paton Walsh's eye. It's a fine book; right in the mainstream of the traditional historical novel, as good as the best of Geoffrey Trease, Henry Treece, and Rosemary Sutcliff.

Unleaving is a sequel to *Goldengrove*, with Madge appearing in two roles, as an eighteen-year-old about to leave school, and, decades later, as a grandmother. Though there is still a tendency to cover the page with too much descriptive writing, it is much more of an achievement than *Goldengrove*; there is a taut gripping narrative, a much deeper probing of character and motive than in her previous novels, and event is allowed to develop out of the meeting and clash of people rather than from a known historical framework. The limitations of the intellectual life, summed up in the barbed satirical comments about the professor and his reading-group of philosophy students, are put beside Madge's more emotional instinctive existence; arid discussions on whether ends justify means are contrasted sharply with the book's great dramatic moment, the mongoloid child, Molly, falling or perhaps being pushed by Patrick over the cliff-edge. *Unleaving* is, on several levels, abouts contrasts: Madge hesitantly falling in love with Patrick (for once Jill Paton Walsh creates a convincing teenage romance) is observed together with Madge as a mature fulfilled woman, enjoying the presence in her house of her grandchildren on holiday; the inexplicable mystery of flat contradictions in people (the professor's love for his mongoloid daughter, seen against the professor as a dry-as-dust philosophy don); the beauty of landscape and of the sea which masks its power to maim and kill; the tendency of memory to distort so that the truth is almost impossible to discern. The impressive opening section, where Madge's grandmother's funeral is interrupted by the launching of the lifeboat and the pallbearers abandon the coffin to join in the rescue, sets the tone for the whole novel: the tension produced in moments of choice and dilemma. The issues discussed in *Unleaving* are all being tackled by teenagers who are facing, for the first time in their lives, adult situations, and the author never puts a foot wrong in showing how well or how badly her adolescents measure up. The dialogue is good; it's used, for once to develop plot and character, not simply to impart information. At last one is not forced to be aware of the novelist breathing down one's neck. There are faults; there is still an inability to create believable working class characters — ◆ 149 Jeremy, the fisherman, is a stock rustic — bronzed, crinkly-faced and forelock-touching. He speaks in a supposedly

Cornish dialect that doesn't begin to sound like the real language spoken in the West of England. But when one considers what skills there are in most of the book, such mistakes seem no more than minor blemishes.

One might have assumed that with *The Emperor's Winding Sheet* and *Unleaving* Jill Paton Walsh had reached maturity as a writer, but the two canal stories, *The Butty Boy* and *A Chance Child*, are a disappointment. *The Butty Boy* (published in America as *The Huffler*) again leaves the most interesting idea undeveloped, as only a hint on the last page. That idea is Harriet's rejection of the chinless drip, Edward, because she hankers after Ned, the working class bargee she met and knew for a few days when she was a child. It has much more potential than the rather hackneyed theme that occupies most of the book; the middle class girl running away and seeing how the other half lives. It's a common enough plot, particularly in Victorian children's novels; Mark Twain's *The Prince and the Pauper* is a typical example. In fact *The Butty Boy* is constructed quite satisfactorily, but without being anything memorable. It's also marred slightly by undigested bits of information about canals, barges, and lock-gates; this is a Paton Walsh fault — characteristic in several books: too much instruction protrudes through the exchanges between John and Pat in *The Dolphin Crossing* when they are discussing Hitler's campaign in the Low Countries, and Pat, somewhat improbably, doesn't know much about the background to the war and needs to be told; and in the conversations between Vrethiki and Stephanos in *The Emperor's Winding Sheet*, it is sometimes Jill Paton Walsh giving an account of Byzantine culture, art, and history, rather than Stephanos doing so.

More disturbing, however, in *The Butty Boy*, is yet another change in the author's style. This time there is a forced simplicity, strings of short phrases joined by conjunctions that make the prose seem out of breath:

Up they came, past the wet masonry of the lock, and into the sweet sun and air again, and found themselves in the middle of a handsome town, with green public gardens, and a fine tall church with a spire, and wide streets thronging with people.

The many adjectives — sweet, handsome, green, fine — could easily be removed without the description losing anything. They are not words that tell us what the town or the church look like; they are there to produce a cozy warmth in the reader. One of the points that the book is trying to make is that working class life in the nineteenth century was hard and the people ill-fed, overworked, and underpaid, but the bargees in *The Butty Boy* are somewhat too jolly and rosy-cheeked: it's the past distorted by nostalgia. While the children are waiting for their horse to be shod "the blacksmith's wife gave them a little round apple pasty each, hot from the oven." In every incident there's something comforting taking the edge off what it was really like.

The subject matter of *A Chance Child* is the deplorable exploitation of child labor in nineteenth century industrial England, a theme as vast in scope and as damning an indictment of a greedy profit-seeking society as the background material of *The Slave Dancer*. The idea has been used before in children's books, most notably by William Rayner, a neglected, much underestimated author, in his very fine novel *Big Mister*. *A Chance Child* is fantasy rather than straight history, moving from past to present, the link being Creep, a ghost who seems to represent all down-trodden exploited children in any age. This gives Jill Paton Walsh the opportunity of concentrating not on one particular story, but on taking us on a guided tour, by canal, round selected examples of various industries and their child workers: coal-mines, a pottery, a textile factory, a steel works. It also leaves her with no time to involve the reader at a deep level; no sooner have we begun to absorb one thing when we're off on another.

There is far too much unrelieved description, much of it reminiscent of the Dickens of *Hard Times*, but lacking his anger and savage satirical bite. The book is written in the same out-of-breath style as *The Butty Boy*; at the end one feels bewildered and dissatisfied. Only once, in this catalogue of horrors, does anything come over as really nasty — the description of the scars on Blackie's face. Apart from that, one is left remarkably unmoved.

Jill Paton Walsh's work is very uneven in quality. Of her eight books, only three — *Hengest's Tale*, *The Emperor's Winding Sheet*, and *Unleaving* — are completely successful, though there are some fine moments in *The Dolphin Crossing* and *Fireweed*. Her novels also raise an important question that can only be described as political: how should we present history to children? A writer cannot help imposing his vision of the world on the material he uses, and Jill Paton Walsh's values seem to be the same as those Fred Inglis, in "Reading Children's Novels: Notes on the Politics of Literature" sees in Rosemary Sutcliff's work: "the present-day accents of the unkillable member of our society since 1800, the Liberal intellectual woman." There is nothing wrong in that, but there is an inconsistency in Jill Paton Walsh's work: her softening of the more unpalatable edges of our past and writing with a nostalgia for our great heroic moments is not "Liberal intellectual" and it is not good for our children to see history so presented. It's all too easy for Madge in *Unleaving* to say, from her comfortable middle class home, surrounded by happy grandchildren, and looking out at the incomparable view of St. Ives Bay, that we should sing "the beauty of the world." It looks rather different from Harlem or Wigan. I'm not suggesting that a Liberal presentation of history — or even a Conservative one — should be replaced by a Marxist version, but I am saying that we should know precisely what we're doing with history before we begin to write historical novels, particularly for children. To encourage a kind of yearning for the Dunkirk spirit is wrong; our problems today can't be dealt with in the terms of 1940. Fred Inglis says Rosemary Sutcliff's novels define a response to

> the loss of the English landscape both in itself and as a symbol of one version of Englishness; they further define a powerful and unfulfilled longing for a richer moral vocabulary and an ampler, more graceful and courteous style of living such as at the present time can only be embodied in a stylized past.

Jill Paton Walsh may well be doing the same kind of thing; one notices it even in *The Emperor's Winding Sheet*, in some of the plangent cadences and rotund rhetoric in which the past is evoked. It worries me: it's a bit like turning one's back on the difficult issues of real life and hoping they'll slip decently away.

References

JILL PATON WALSH

> *Hengest's Tale* Macmillan, London, 1966; St. Martin 1966
> *The Dolphin Crossing* Macmillan, London, 1967; St. Martin 1967
> *Fireweed* Macmillan, London, 1969; Farrar 1970
> *Goldengrove* Macmillan, London, 1972; Farrar 1972
> *The Emperor's Winding Sheet* Macmillan, London, 1974; Farrar 1974
> *The Butty Boy* Macmillan, London, 1975; Farrar 1975 (as *The Huffler*)
> *Unleaving* Macmillan, London, 1976; Farrar 1976
> *A Chance Child* Macmillan, London, 1978, Farrar 1978

PHILIPPA PEARCE

> *Tom's Midnight Garden* Oxford 1958; Lippincott 1959

PAULA FOX

> *The Stone-Faced Boy* Bradbury 1968; Macmillan, London, 1969

The Slave Dancer Bradbury 1973; Macmillan, London, 1974

ROBERT WESTALL
The Machine Gunners Macmillan, London, 1975; Greenwillow 1976

NINA BAWDEN
Carrie's War Gollancz 1973; Lippincott 1973

PENELOPE LIVELY
Going Back Heinemann 1975; Dutton 1975

DAVID JAMES
"Recent World-War-II Fiction" in *Children's literature in education*, Summer 1977

VIRGINIA WOOLF
To the Lighthouse first published in 1927

MARK TWAIN
The Prince and the Pauper first published in 1881

CHARLES DICKENS
Hard Times first published in 1854

WILLIAM RAYNER
Big Mister Collins, London, 1974

FRED INGLIS
"Reading Children's Novels: Notes on the Politics of Literature" in *Children's literature in education*, July 1971

The Sadness
of Compromise

◆

ROBERT CORMIER
and JILL CHANEY

IN RECENT YEARS novels for the young adult have
proliferated so much that one could almost call this particular market a growth industry, even though authors
seem to have gone out of their way to stress the problems
adolescents may be confronted by rather than the excite-
ments and pleasures of this period of life. Unwanted
pregnancies, drugs, abortion, crime and unsatisfactory
parents all occur more frequently in teenage fiction than
happy home backgrounds, fulfilling love affairs, or indeed
the average preoccupations of most young people. One
may easily sympathize with readers who vainly search
for something that reflects life as they know it.

One lesson that must be learned in the teenage years
is that it is often necessary to compromise in order to
survive; that the gap between the actual and the ideal has
to be bridged; that, as Ben Blewitt comes to realize in
Philippa Pearce's *A Dog So Small*, "if you didn't have the
possible things, then you had nothing." Too often the hero
in the teenage novel blames a malevolent hostile world
for shortcomings that are his own, and emerges at the
end of the story still convinced that he should turn his
back on things rather than examine his own failings.
Valuable, then, is the work of writers such as Robert
Cormier and Jill Chaney, admittedly quite unlike in style,
preoccupation, and achievement, but who are both con-

cerned with the essential sadness of the inevitable passing from innocence to experience — the compromise of survival. Teenagers need to be able to say, "yes: so that's how you cope with it" and novels that *show them how* are likely to be more helpful to the imaginative and emotional growth of the young people than those that take issues — drugs, venereal disease, or whatever — as starting points.

The Chocolate War, Robert Cormier's first novel for young adults, is, on the surface, a political book. It is about power, power structures, corruption — about how absolute power corrupts absolutely. But, more subtly, beneath the surface, it is about compromise and the choice between hunting with the pack or searching for strength as an individual: about the toughness needed in the struggle to be a successful outsider. Jerry Renault, the central character, is a fascinating and complex creation, considerably more ambiguous than he initially appears to be. One may like him up to a point, and admire his heroic, if futile, refusal to join in the attempts that Brother Leon has organized to raise funds for his school by the sale of the chocolates. There is a strong temptation on the reader's part to identify with him, to agree with his version of events: but it's a temptation that should be resisted. There is much that it not admirable about Jerry Renault. His weakness is an overriding passion to conform to a conventional teenage image of machismo, which is seen mostly in his desire to become an admired member of the football team — looked up to, respected, a boy with a niche in society. He doesn't have any realization that such values are false; that conventional respect from others is no measure of real worth. A similar falseness exists in his attitude to the opposite sex; he wants a relationship with a girl not because it may be more interesting and satisfying than a friendship with another boy, but because

> The one devastating sorrow he carried within him was the fear that he would die before holding a girl's breast in his hand.

He is not the stuff of which heroes are made, and his
final compromise is not the gesture of despair that some
critics have suggested, but entirely characteristic:

> He had to tell Goober to play ball, to play football, to
> run, to make the team, to sell the chocolates, to sell
> whatever they wanted you to sell, to do whatever they
> wanted you to do... Don't disturb the universe,
> Goober, no matter what the posters say.

His stand against selling the chocolates is an aberra-
tion, quite uncharacteristic of him, and it is interesting
that Cormier does not give the reader an adequate explanation for Jerry's decision to opt out in this matter. Goober
is much more naturally an outsider type than Jerry, and
though his appearance in the book is disappointingly fleet-
ing, Cormier would have manufactured a much less worth-
while novel if he had made Goober the central character
for it would have become a rather conventional struggle
between good and evil.

The Chocolate War is not an entirely satisfactory
book. Goober is not the only person left undeveloped; the
author shows us the thinking processes of too many of his
characters, and he flits more rapidly than he should from
one to another; the writing is at times too purple, especially
in the scenes of physical violence. One wonders if the
author may be enjoying these scenes a little, and, I feel,
he may also share Jerry's belief in a false idea of masculine
values. (Robert Westall's novels also leave the reader with
a similar uncomfortable sensation.) The evil characters,
Archie and Brother Leon, are so one-dimensionally
villainous that they are no more than caricatures. They
present a considerable threat to the reader's ability to
believe in the reality of what he is being told. But the
central theme – to conform or not to conform – is handled
with great skill, and the book's message is more subtle
than it seems: Cormier is not saying that the might of ♦ 157
evil institutions inevitably corrupts good people, but that
the desire to be accepted is a major weakness which can

easily be exploited by the wicked. *The Chocolate War* is a very popular book with teenagers in England as well as in America, and on the whole deservedly so.

There is little obvious compromise in *I Am the Cheese*, for political power and corruption are not illustrated in this book through the world of school life, but by the power of the government itself, and Cormier's message here is much more bleak: that the stand of one or two individuals against the whole apparatus of government is hopeless. Adam, the central character, is someone we might find in many novels for young adults, a teenager who is struggling to find — on many levels — who he is and what his place in the world should be. We see his first meaningful love affair and we explore the complexities of his feelings for his parents; but what makes Adam's situation different from that of the hero in almost all teenage fiction is that the reader knows, at the end of the book, that he is going to die; either he will be "terminated" as his parents were, or the treatment he is receiving in a psychiatric hospital will "obliterate" him. Complaints by critics that the hopelessness of *I Am the Cheese* is inappropriate to a story for young people are not justifiable in my opinion; there is no good reason why a teenage novel should not express total despair: the young do not have to be protected in this way. And there are parts of this novel which, by any standards, are far from hopeless — Adam's relationship with his father, for example, is a rare thing in today's fiction for the young: there is love, care, thoughtfulness, and admiration on both sides. Indeed it is a model of what such relationships should be, despite the evidence presented in too many novels.

The writing is excellent throughout; none of the faults that mar *The Chocolate War* are to be seen in 158 ◆ *I Am the Cheese*. The prose has a very positive sound to it; an appealing music in its cadences; an appropriateness in its images:

> So they drove and his father recited some fragments of Thomas Wolfe, about October and the tumbling leaves of bitter red, or yellow leaves like living light, and Adam was sad again, thinking of his father as a writer and how his life had changed, how it had become necessary for him to give up all that and become another person altogether, how all of them had become other persons, his father, his mother, and himself. Paul Delmonte, poor lost Paul Delmonte.

In such a passage as this is the kind of compromise that is not obvious, because it lies beneath the surface of the narrative: Adam sadly accepting that the fugitive existence to which he and his parents have been reduced is inevitable. *I Am the Cheese* is a much better book than *The Chocolate War*; the explanations revealed at the end are quite shattering, and the author's skill in concealing them until this point is immense. The structure, in fact, is very satisfying throughout. Technical expertise and the quality of the writing are of equal merit. It's a pity that it is not as widely read as *The Chocolate War*, but the reason is easy to see: it's much more difficult, requiring a quite different order of intelligence in the reader.

After the First Death has the same skills as *I Am the Cheese*; tension, conveyed fear, ability to write a narrative so exciting that the reader is gripped completely, but it is not a book that breaks new ground or that extends Cormier's range. It is undoubtedly very good, probably the best of the spate of novels about terrorism and hi-jacking that have appeared in recent years, though Cormier has serious competition from Farrukh Dhondy in *The Siege of Babylon* and James Hamilton-Paterson in *Hostage!* Where it scores higher than similar stories do is in the exploration of the weaknesses of the victims — the General's willingness to put country before family even when he knows it will destroy his son's self-respect; Kate Forrester's realization that her only weapon in the struggle is to use her sexual attractiveness; Ben's inability to come to terms with both his own supposed cowardice and the fact that his father has cold-bloodedly exploited that cowardice as a pawn in the bargaining game with the hi-jackers. Once again, the young — Kate, Ben, and the sixteen-year-old terrorist, Miro — are forced to compromise. Some of them, Cormier suggests, can survive with their integrity intact: Kate does so (though minutes later she is killed) and the new aspects of himself that Miro discovers are rapidly suppressed, so strong is the power of his upbringing. Yet Ben goes under, irrevocably maimed, and in him lies the real tragedy of the story: compromise totally destroys him.

Cormier, in this novel, questions some fundamental beliefs — the commonplace views of patriotism, of cowardice and courage, of the expectations of both parties in father-son relationships. (Miro's relationship with Artkin exactly parallels that of Ben and his father, and all four are seen to be guilty of false assumptions about the nature of such relationships — assumptions that are the products of conditioning and prove inadequate when put to the test.) Very interesting, too, is his suggestion that although innocence in itself is good and valuable, it is a severely limited concept — dangerous and even outrageous:

> He had seduced her with his pathetic tale of wandering through the camps as a child and had somehow enlisted her sympathy. But now she recognized him for what he was: a monster. And the greatest horror of all was that he did not know he was a monster. He had looked at her with innocent eyes as he told her of killing people. She'd always thought of innocence as something good, something to cherish. People mourned the death of innocence. Someone had written a theme paper

on the topic in school. But innocence, she saw now, could also be evil. Monstrous.

How good a novelist is Cormier? His work is greeted with almost hysterical praise by reviewers. He is compared with Bellow, Styron, Salinger, Golding; it's almost as if critics had never before seen real talent in authors of young adult novels. The comparisons do not hold up, of course. Consider his work and that of Saul Bellow and Cormier is seen at once to have obvious limitations, particularly in the narrowness of his chosen area, for the situations in his books are always extreme: no one is ever observed in the middle of the processes of ordinary living. The relationships he writes about are also limited, indeed repetitive — father and son, manipulator and pawn. Kate is the only female character in the three books who is explored in depth. The themes of *After the First Death* are much the same as *I Am the Cheese* and *The Chocolate War* — the corruptness of authoritarian institutions and people; the violence and destruction they engender. The most disappointing characteristic of *After the First Death* is that, though remarkably well done, it appears to be going over the same ground again. Nor is there a feeling in his work, as there is in that of Jill Chaney, of the immense variety and richness of human experience, for while the dramas and tragedies he writes of are, to say the least, unusual, they are certainly not those that the vast majority of people will experience in the course of a lifetime. Good, yes: he *is* a very good writer: but it is far too soon to reach for superlatives of praise.

Jill Chaney's revelation of compromise is of an absolutely opposite nature to Robert Cormier's even though the passage quoted above from *I Am the Cheese* sounds remarkably like her tone of voice. There is nothing political in her novels, no dramatic plots, and not a great deal happens other than the usual routines of the suburban English middle-class world (where she seems most at home) and of the rural working class in *The Buttercup Field*. Sheila takes typing lessons; Gary visits France, alone on his motorbike; a domineering old grandmother dies. There are, it is true, a few oddities: a peculiar uncle who lives in a hut on the East Coast; Mr. Evans, who unexpectedly leaves his wife to live with another woman; Dick's encounter with some petty thieves in London. But, on the whole, the even monotonous pace of everyday living ticks on in the foreground, and behind it we are constantly aware of what Ralph, Gary, Sheila, and Dick think and feel. For most of the time we are inside their heads and hearts, exploring, muddling, analyzing, and almost always compromising: compromising between what they feel they are; what they feel for boy friend or girl friend; what they long to be and do; and the dull grey reality of what is expected of them by the dictates of the ordinary normal adult world.

Half a Candle was something of a break-through when it was published in 1968. Catherine Storr, answering a question at the Exeter Conference in 1969, said that it was the only novel she knew of that dealt realistically and well with a teenage love affair. It was a book enthusiastically reviewed and widely read by children's literature experts, and the only one of her books to be published in the United States,* but it never seemed to filter through to the teenagers themselves. Not enough teachers knew about it, and it has never been published in paperback. (Indeed, none of Jill Chaney's novels has appeared in paperback and the opportunity of making them available to a wider audience is long overdue.) Maybe *Half a Candle* didn't fit into a

---

* Jill Chaney refused an offer from Harper to publish *Mottram Park* in America as so many alterations to the British edition were requested that she felt the book was no longer hers. It is a great pity that American readers were denied the chance of discovering the pleasures of this very fine novel, but I'm sure Jill Chaney was quite right in her decision. It's high time some Americans stopped complaining that British novels contain "too many British expressions" and started to enjoy the differences.

convenient slot, being neither a children's book nor an adult book, though it is hard to see why it was not brought out in the Peacock series. Later, when paperbacks for teenagers became more common, it had probably been forgotten.

The story is quite simple. Ralph, half-English and half-Malay, comes to England for the first time at the age of fifteen; his father has recently died, and he is offered a home with relatives in Twickenham. The way of life of suburban London he finds intolerable, and his uncle and aunt and cousins are insensitive and dull. So he goes to live with another uncle, an eccentric bachelor, Adrian, who lives alone in the Suffolk marshes. Here Ralph begins to feel happy; he works on a farm, potato-picking and sawing wood, and the great open spaces of the landscape and sky of the Alde estuary he finds far more congenial than shut-in Twickenham. He meets an American girl of his own age (her father is stationed at an airbase nearby) and they fall in love. The depth of feeling and the hopeless impossibility of its leading to anything that will last are what the author stresses in particular. Ralph and Lesley take a boat out on the estuary, walk in the marshes, go one night to a dance. Out of the blue, the Twickenham relations arrive and take Ralph away with them. Uncle Adrian cannot, or will not, look after him permanently.

Not a very exciting plot, as I said, but it has a perfect shape. Its mood is best summed up by Uncle Adrian's remark:

> Don't you realize that probably seventy-five per cent of people exist in an uncomprehending state of partial unhappiness? Or perhaps it would be a lot more accurate to say that a lot of people are discontented most of the time.

The mood is exactly mirrored by the flat grey landscape, which is present, hauntingly, throughout much of the book, but Ralph, in love, is able to escape, if only fleetingly, from this "partial unhappiness," not only when Lesley is actually present, but when he is working and anticipating the next meeting.

> He was aware, dimly, that Millie's sister wanted him to talk to her, to like her, to respond in some way, but he felt strange and half-dissolved himself. "Yes," he said, or "no." Or "gosh, do you?" And then Millie's sister touched his arm and went, it seemed sadly, back to the house. He was alone for a moment, intensely aware of the field gate ahead of him, the grass under his flapping shoes — he could actually feel it with his toes, quite cool and earthy in spite of the heat — and the hum of birds and small insects, and aeroplanes in the distance, which together, created a kind of orchestra. But all the afternoon, the potatoes; until he was back in his muffled haze, half-alive, almost perhaps a potato himself, he thought, wondering at their smooth skins. Like silk outside, and yet, occasionally, when he found one that had been cut by the plough, rough and wet and earthy inside.

But cruel reality conquers in the end. As Lesley says,

> That's the awful thing about being a child. I mean, it's meant to be the happiest days of your life and all that, but it isn't. Because you're not free. I don't mean I want to be free to do anything awful; I just want to be responsible for myself, and not to be told what's reasonable and what isn't. Anyway my parents are really quite nice.

The same low-key atmosphere pervades *Mottram Park* and its sequel, *Return to Mottram Park*, but the beauty of Suffolk is replaced by a drab outer-London suburb which

> has no character . . . There is a road where shops are situated, but no faces, no pubs, no communal meeting places, nothing that would promote some social life for the young amongst the population. Their parents either

feel no need for it, their entertainment needs being adequately supplied by television, or they meet in each other's houses to play whist.

But the relationship between Gary, who is nearly seventeen, and Sheila, who is fifteen, is a much more possible one than that between Ralph and Lesley — possible in the sense of not being abruptly broken off by circumstances. A triumph of both books is Gary, one of the most convincingly real male youths in contemporary teenage fiction; there is not a hint of him being an impossible invention of a female author's imagination. Jill Chaney manages to convey exactly what is it like to be a complex and sensitive boy of seventeen, and it is an unusual achievement to get so thoroughly inside the mind, emotions, and instincts of the opposite sex as she does. Gary is a gruff, slightly introverted person, who is at his happiest with his motorbike, but relaxed with his parents, intelligent and academically bright, very self-sufficient in some ways. Sheila is a weaker person, dominated by her parents and her grandmother, less bright, rather clinging; she sees Gary almost as a godlike figure. He finds her adoration of him rather off-putting, and though he is more than half in love with her, he shies away from the commitment she seems to be demanding. He looks forward to adulthood as being equated with freedom, the room to explore and discover who he is and what is important, and in no way wishes to be tied down by Sheila, who may unconsciously be using him as a way of freeing herself from her dreary family.

The differences in feeling that each has for the other are well-illustrated by the concluding paragraphs of the first and second chapters. In the first, Gary is lying in bed thinking of Sheila; in the second she is thinking of him. For Gary it is a slight nuisance that Sheila is in his mind, for he is trying to concentrate on an article in a motor-cycling magazine; on the other hand Sheila has pushed all other thoughts out of her head so that she can think only of Gary. It is neatly ironic, for Gary succeeds in seeing her much more clearly than she does him, whereas he comes into her head as someone not unlike the hero in a romance, a fact that the author clearly wishes to convey to the reader, for the clichés stand out with a nice humor. These are Gary's thoughts:

> It would be more difficult, he thought, if there were two of you in a bed. There'd be bound to be draughts. But he supposed there'd be sufficient compensations to outweigh this disadvantage. She was a funny kid — Sheila. She looked so bloody cross half the time, and you felt she wasn't really. She was putting it on to show off, or to defend herself or something. Perhaps she'd take him in one day to meet her family. Perhaps she'd got one of those old-fashioned fathers, as she had to be in by half past ten. But the only person he'd actually heard her grumble about was her grandmother. He paused to reflect on her appearance before he went back to The Road Test Report. She hadn't grown her hair as long as some did, and it curled up at the ends. She wore a white hair band like a kid, but it looked all right on her with that black hair. She had blue eyes and a nice little face. She was small; he couldn't stand those great hefty birds with massive legs. He saw her laugh in his mind's eye, and then she was gone, while he tried to conjure her back into vision. But it was no good, and he resumed his reading.

Here is Sheila thinking of Gary:

> She loved to lie in the dark and think of Gary. She would think of what he had said, how he had looked, whether he had kissed her. He did sometimes, but always briefly and casually, as though his mind was on something else. She saw him in her mind's eye, bent over his precious motor bike, standing back to admire it, frowning slightly if he thought the tyre pressures needed adjusting. He had such a kind face. He didn't look like most of the boys you saw around. He thought about other things than motor bikes or sleeping with girls

too. He considered things. Perhaps it was studying Mathematics? He was cleverer than most of the boys she knew. She sighed and slipped further as she concocted one of her daydreams in which Gary declared undying love for her, and carried her off on his motor bike, and they were terribly, terribly happy together.

The contrast — his being diffident, more involved than he realizes, slightly patronizing, more overtly sexual, versus her unreal, fuzzy romanticism — becomes the area of conflict between the two throughout the book and its sequel.

Again, nothing much happens in *Mottram Park*. Gary's sister, Angela, has a brief and unhappy affair with a married man, and swallows an overdose of sleeping pills. She recovers in hospital. Sheila's nasty grandmother, at the end of the book, has a stroke. These are the only moments of drama, apart from a violent quarrel Sheila has with her family, which leads her, on the spur of the moment, to run away from home. She lives for a few days in a deserted bungalow by the Thames; Gary visits her, and, on one occasion, they try to make love. It is a failure — there are too many tensions; it is the first time for either of them; they are worried about not using contraceptives — and Gary feels terribly humiliated by his inability to do anything. But despite the failure, there is relief that it didn't actually happen as they consider the possible consequences, and a real tenderness between them. Gary takes Sheila back to her parents, but from then on, the relationship begins to disintegrate. He broods on his failure, and she finds his lack of sympathy about the news of her grandmother's stroke infuriating and depressing. Suddenly, he is no longer a god-like figure on a pedestal. They drift apart.

Yet sad though it all sounds, they have one long day of perfect happiness, the first time Gary takes her on the back of his motorbike to the river. They do nothing more exciting than take a boat out for a couple of hours, but both are in perfect harmony with one another and their surroundings: free, for once, of parents, school, responsibilities, dull old Mottram Park. It is a memory that stays with Sheila throughout much of the sequel, *Return to Mottram Park*. They're both a year older; Gary is taking "A" levels and Sheila has left school to work as a secretary in an estate agent's office. They meet accidentally and try, for much of the book, to pick up the pieces. But Sheila's dumb worship (as Gary sees it) still bothers him; he takes his motorbike to France for a long, solitary holiday, and only writes to her once. He meets a beautiful German girl and spends the night with her. Because it is such a casual encounter he is without tension, and he is rid, once and for all, of fears of sexual inadequacy. But when, next morning, the girl leaves him, pointing out that they are traveling in opposite directions (he is returning to England; she is heading for the South of France) he feels humiliated in a different way. He had hoped it would be the start of a new, marvelous relationship.

> Never, since as a very small boy he had been unintentionally rude to a favorite uncle and received the united fury of his parents and the uncle, had he felt so small and unloved. . . . Crumpled and sad he sat for a while on the uneven sand where the tent had rested, picking up the odd handful of the stuff and letting it run through his fingers. Hell, he thought, Hell! What was the point of anything?

He returns home, discovers that he has passed his exams well enough to take up his university place, and goes out to find Sheila.

> She had always been there when he needed her. He had hankered after her, on and off, for two years. She obviously adored him. Why should he look any further?

168 ◆ On the spur of the moment, he asks her to marry him. Is he falling into a trap he really wants to avoid? The book ends with an enigmatic exchange of dialogue:

"Don't go mooning about sloppily, thinking I'm marvellous. It wouldn't be good for either of us."

"I'll try," she said, a little puzzled. Gary himself wondered why he had said it, but kissing again, they both forgot it.

The ability to make the very ordinary come alive, to make it really compelling is where Jill Chaney's success lies. In the detail, the varying shades of emotion, the questions, puzzles, discoveries of the self and of each other, Gary and Sheila have few equals in contemporary teenage fiction.

The inside of his head might have been a washing machine, he thought, with disconnected items tumbling about in it and being elbowed aside by the one behind.

So it may seem at sixteen or seventeen, but Jill Chaney shows, for the discerning reader, exactly how all the items are in fact connected.

Dick, in *The Buttercup Field*, is fifteen, a slow farmer's son in rural Oxfordshire. His horizons are the village he has always lived in, the seasonal occupations of the farm, the occasional trip to Oxford to a disco with friends of both sexes whom he has known all his life. As the book opens, he is thoroughly unsettled by the recent death of his brother Ray in a motorbike accident: then a writer and his family from London move into a nearby house; there is a daughter, Jessica, and Dick falls in love with her. She likes him, but is puzzled and a bit frightened by his feelings; and she is highly embarrassed when he gives her a present that is very expensive, a brooch with a red and blue enamel kingfisher on a background made of silver. Her parents disapprove, and think she should not accept the gift. Dick, confused, desperately unhappy, and still extremely upset by his brother's death, runs away to London, where he lives at first with some hippy layabouts, then in the house of an Italian couple who own a restaurant where he finds work, doing the washing-up. The police trace him and take him back

◆ 169

home. The last third of the book shows him trying to come to terms with the consequences of these experiences. His family is, with the exception of his older brother, Bob, bewildered and saddened, which Dick finds harder to cope with than outright anger or punishment. But he attempts to make a fresh start with Jessica. He finds he can now keep the intensity of his passion under control; he begins to see that his feelings for her are not the be-all and end-all of everything, but part of a developing pattern of feeling that must include his family, friends, and school; and the book ends on an optimistic note, when she agrees, for the first time, to go out with him the following Saturday.

The Buttercup Field is in some ways a return to the earlier manner of *Half a Candle*; falling in love here has no yardsticks, no reasonableness or maturity with which it can be moderated, and it is therefore absurd and a little frightening.

"You don't like me," he said angrily. "Not at all. Otherwise you'd come."

"It's not like that," she said tearfully. "I do like you. Of course I like you."

He should not have given her the kingfisher brooch. He should have said nothing. He had frightened her, he had alarmed her family. Had it shown on his face, what he felt? They all knew too much now. But how had they known, just from the brooch?

"I'll go," he said angrily, flinging himself away. "It's all a lot of silly fuss."

He walked away, refusing to allow himself to turn round, into the gold and orange evening. Would he ever, he thought mournfully, enjoy days like this again? Clean, pure summer evenings with bees still busy collecting their supper from the fragrant hedges and house martins overhead and the cool breezes of the night creeping round: Would he ever again be able to disconnect these memories from the humiliation of Jessica rejecting him?

But things are not brought to an abrupt halt as in *Half a Candle*. The time span is longer, and Dick has enough room to grow up a little. Whether his relationship with Jessica will succeed or not is not the point; he is older and a little wiser, and won't make the same mistakes twice. "The whole of life," he says to himself, "seemed to be one vast uneasy compromise."

The American author who comes nearest to Jill Chaney in portraying the details of the ordinary world of the small-town middle class teenager is Beverly Cleary. *Fifteen*, written nearly a quarter of a century ago, is still immensely popular; in England the paperback edition has been reprinted fifteen times since its first appearance in 1963. All too often this novel has been dismissed as superior girls' magazine fiction, but it is high time tribute was paid to Beverly Cleary's merits: *Fifteen* has a fine narrative pace, considerable wit, accurate insight into the feelings and motives of its central character, and the writing is individual, indeed stylish. It's wonderfully dated, of course, with its girls finding boys' crew-cuts sexy, and its rigidly separated male-female roles: boys walking on the outsides of pavements and opening car doors for their girl friends, et cetera. Barbara Cartland would approve no end. But this is unimportant, merely the trivia of life in 1956. What is so good is the truth with which Beverly Cleary records the teenager's anguish and joy, in *any* period, about things that an adult accepts easily enough or doesn't have to struggle with: the problems, for instance, of eating food you don't like when your boy friend is paying for it; of persuading parents you're quite safe in your boy friend's car; of acne and hair-dos and not having anything suitable to wear. Jane Purdy's problems are, in the great ultimate, mere pin-pricks; they are hardly on the scale of the problems faced by Robert Cormier's heroes, or, for that matter, of Jill Chaney's more contemporary young people; but at fifteen the question of whether to stand up or sit down when

The Sadness of Compromise

your boy friend arrives at your house for the first time can seem insurmountable. Maybe the author should have introduced a few real problems; maybe Stan Crandall with his lovely green eyes is a misty feminine creation, but the whole business of falling in love at fifteen — a moony, walking-on-air, ridiculously romantic kind of falling in love — is in this book completely authentic: the compromises have yet to come.

It is a pity that authors so similar in some ways as Beverly Cleary and Jill Chaney should differ so much in their popularity. Authors who can create people in all their living complexities so well that the reader says again and again: "yes, that's true," are worth serious consideration anywhere, whether they are as well-known as Robert Cormier and Beverly Cleary or as neglected as Jill Chaney.

References

ROBERT CORMIER
The Chocolate War Pantheon 1974; Gollancz 1975
I Am the Cheese Pantheon 1977; Gollancz 1977
After the First Death Pantheon 1979; Gollancz 1979

JILL CHANEY
Half a Candle Dobson 1968; Crown 1969
Mottram Park Dobson 1970
Return to Mottram Park Dobson 1974
The Buttercup Field Dobson 1977

BEVERLY CLEARY
Fifteen Morrow 1956; Penguin 1963

FARRUKH DHONDY
The Siege of Babylon Macmillan, London, 1978

JAMES HAMILTON-PATERSON
Hostage! Gollancz 1978

PHILIPPA PEARCE
A Dog So Small Constable 1962; Lippincott 1963

CATHERINE STORR
answer to a question at the Exeter, England, Conference on children's literature 1969

Not Even for
a One-Night Stand

◆

JUDY BLUME

To TURN from the novels of Jill Chaney to those of Judy Blume is like exchanging a caress for a bashing on the head with a blunt instrument. Perhaps the best thing to do with Ms. Blume would be to ignore her altogether; she is so amazingly trivial and second-rate in every department — the quality of her English, her ability to portray character, to unfold narrative but that is impossible: she is "controversial" on both sides of the Atlantic, and her work is read and discussed not only by the young but by those adults who have a serious concern for children's literature. Four of her books have recently appeared in England, accompanied by a great blaze of publicity. But English paperback editions of her novels do not include *Forever*, I'm glad to say, and that particular story has not sold at all well in Britain, where it is published on a teenage list. It's curious that in the United States it was published as "Judy Blume's first novel for adults," for the teenage market would certainly seem to be Judy Blume's target.

What sort of picture would a being from another planet form of teenage and pre-teenage America were he able to read *Are You There, God? It's Me, Margaret* and *Forever*? He would imagine that youth was obsessed with bras, period pains, deodorants, orgasms, and family planning; that life was a great race to see who was first to get laid or to use a Tampax; that childhood and adolescence were unpleasant obstacles on the road to adulthood —

◆ 173

periods (sorry!) of life to be raced through as quickly as possible, to be discarded as casually as Michael in *Forever* throws away his used contraceptive. He would discover that the young have almost no intellect and very few feelings; that falling in love is not a matter of complex emotions that seem at the time to change one's perception of people — indeed the whole world — out of all recognition; but that it is simply a question of should one go on the pill or not, swapping partners quite heartlessly, and whether one is doing it right in bed. He'd realize, with some surprise, that sex isn't even very erotic: that it's just clinical.

Adolescents do of course have period pains and worry about the size of their breasts or penises; they fall in love and some of them sleep together. There should obviously be a place for all these concerns in teenage novels; but to write about them, as Judy Blume does, to the exclusion of everything else is doing youth a great disservice. She succeeds quite magnificently in trivializing everything, particularly young people themselves. She would appear not to know that they do find time, whatever their emotional and sexual preoccupations may be, to be interested in and participate in a very wide spectrum of human existence. To serve them up the kind of stuff of which *Forever* consists is to underestimate totally their ability to think and to feel, not only about themselves but about the whole complexity of living that goes on around them.

Nor is that Judy Blume's only major fault. *Forever* has a bad taste, a want of sensibility, a heavy-handed clumsiness that is breath-taking. The reader's reaction is laughter — anything from an embarrassed snigger to falling out of a chair with hilarity — when he ought to feel moved or excited or enthralled. Instead of enjoying one of the most rewarding of experiences, that of being so wrapped up in reading a novel that one loses, for a while, all form of engagement with anything outside the book, one is irresistibly urged to read the next excruciating paragraph aloud to family or friends so that they can all join in the fun.

Consider the artless banality of this: "I came right before Michael and as I did I made noises, just like my mother." It's the same sort of language as "I went into the kitchen and fixed myself a cup of coffee." Most writers are aware that human activity is enormously rich and varied, and to give value to that variety, what is linguistically apt for one thing is inappropriate to another. But not so Judy Blume. She has no sense of the incongruous, not even a sense of humor. There may be people who use after-shave lotion in the manner Kath suggests to Michael — on his balls — but were such a topic to arise in conversation, either in real life or in a novel, it would usually be treated as something grotesque or, at the very least, amusing; not by Judy Blume, however: it's done in the same tone as everything else in the book. Of course it makes the reader laugh, but that is something one assumes she didn't intend to do — and it isn't the kind of laughter she would like.

One could go on with other examples, but it hardly seems worth it. It's enough to say that the triviality of her thinking is matched by the sheer shoddiness of her English. She employs the usual sub-Salingerese American first-person narration, but so unmemorably that it makes Paul Zindel's use of the technique look like startling originality. There is absolutely nothing in Judy Blume's style that defines it as specifically hers. Nicholas Tucker, in a review of *Forever* in the *Times Literary Supplement*, said that "talking straight from the adolescent's mouth can act as camouflage for slack writing" — indeed it all too often does — and added that Judy Blume's prose was "of the same soggy consistency as the used tissues that play such an important part in Kath's and Michael's post-amatory techniques." There is an implication here that the English has a built-in throw-away quality to it, that it is as disposable as the used tissue itself. Nicholas Tucker is right; ◆ 175

Judy Blume's novels are the ultimate in the read-it-and-throw-it-away kind of book. They seem to be saying that when you've read the text you'll be equipped to do the real thing and you won't have to bother with the tedious business of coming back to a story to find out what it's like. In other words, they are not only short-changing the young; they are short-changing literature.

Jill Paton Walsh when asked on one occasion why she didn't write a novel on a subject such as a girl having her first period, replied somewhat testily that she wouldn't dream of doing any such thing: It would be a very bad book. Fiction, she said, quite rightly, had its origin in something rather more complex than a given subject, that its genesis was so complex that it was ultimately indefinable. It was certainly not just a matter of one conscious preoccupation, but of all sorts of subconscious concerns of which the author was not fully aware and over which he had little control. However, Judy Blume in *Are You There, God? It's Me, Margaret* rushed in where Jill Paton Walsh very wisely refused to tread, and produced exactly what Jill Paton Walsh foresaw: a very bad book. It's as throwaway as *Forever*. The young reader learns about how to wear a bra and what it's like to have a period, and nothing else is offered that could induce her (a boy is unlikely to find anything in the story of any interest) to return to it and re-open its pages. As for the adult, it's a bore and an embarrassment, a complete waste of one's time.

The trouble stems primarily from thinking that issues — such as how to get laid or what to do when you have your first period — are starting points for creative writing. They are not, and never can be. *Otherwise Known as Sheila the Great* is a marginally better book than *Forever* or *Are You There, God? It's Me, Margaret* because the issues — Sheila Tubman's various phobias about water and dogs — are made secondary considerations to the story, thin though the narrative is. *Tales of a Fourth Grade*

Nothing should also be more interesting for the same reasons, though any attraction it may have is cancelled out by the wretched young brother, a character the author clearly finds very appealing but who comes over to the reader as extremely tiresome. He's a common enough figure in many second-rate children's books; a similar version of the type surfaces in Constance Greene's *I Know You, Al*, another non-novel, or "issue" book, which is also about having one's first period, and, in case that is not enough, divorce as well, with problems looming so large that they squeeze out everything else — story-line, characterization, even good English. Judy Blume's *It's Not the End of the World* is also about divorce, which is certainly a more interesting subject than menstruation. Clash of personalities, disruption of lives, emotional crises, are implicit in the material. It's probably her best book, though what I really mean is that it isn't as bad as the others. Certainly the reactions of the central character, Karen, to the break-up of her parents' marriage seem to ring true. Her sad attempts to bring the adults together again, and her facility for blaming herself when what happens isn't her fault at all, are characteristic of young children who have to suffer in such situations. Authentic, too, is her misunderstanding of trivial actions: she misinterprets them as being of great significance — imagining, for instance, that because her mother has gone to see the same lawyer twice she must be going to marry him. The inability of even the most well-meaning adults to explain what is going on when a marriage collapses, in terms that a child can comprehend, is also well done. But this is not sufficient. The narrator (it's yet another first-person story) sounds as if she is exactly the same person as the narrators in all Judy Blume's books; it could easily be Kath or Margaret, or Vic of *Then Again, Maybe I Won't*. There's an astonishing incapacity to show that people are different from one another in the way they ♦ 177 think and feel and talk: it isn't good enough to suggest that they only differ in their actions. And there is the same entirely forgettable, drab, flat prose:

> We went to visit Daddy's new apartment. He moved this week. The place is called Country Village and it has the kind of streets running through it where you can get lost pretty easy because everything looks the same. There are two swimming pools. One for Country Village East and one for Country Village West. Each section has four apartments. Daddy's is in building 12, upstairs on the right. It's all fixed up like a magazine picture. Everything is brown-and-white and very modern.

Not only is it ungrammatical — "easy" used as an adverb — but this kind of English, pared of all adornment, of anything that is colorful or stimulating or imaginative, sounds like someone trying to explain the most simple things of life to a non-English-speaking foreigner, and is about as exciting to read as the prose of a shopping list.

Then Again, Maybe I Won't is yet another non-novel, the problem this time being what happens if your father suddenly becomes very rich and the whole family moves out of a friendly close-knit lower-middle-class environment to an exceedingly well-to-do suburb, with different rituals, mores, and customs. It isn't a problem that many children are likely to face, but maybe the intention here is to say that life in the smart, private swimming-pool set is so awful in the way it corrupts Mum and Dad that would-be readers will stop hoping their fathers will suddenly find endless riches at their disposal. Whatever the intention is, and it isn't very clear, existence in the upper income bracket really isn't much like this. The *nouveaux riches'* treatment of Grandma, for example, is so callous as to be quite unbelievable, especially when the family background is Italian and Italians are noted for their close-knit family life style. The next-door neighbors are a pretty unattractive crowd, and are so obviously unpalatable to both the reader and the narrator, that it is not easy to see why Vic's mother should wish to imitate them so slavishly. Vic, as one comes to expect in a Judy Blume novel, talks in the usual shopping-list English:

> My bedroom is at the opposite side of the house from my mother and father's. Grandma's is in the middle. I have three windows in my room. Two overlook the backyard and one overlooks the side by the garage. I think the reason we have this circular driveway is so you won't get tired walking from the garage to the front door.
>
> From my two back windows I can see my next-door neighbor's yard. It has a big wooden fence all round it. The kind you can't see through at all if you're on the ground. But from my room I can see right over it.

Nancy Chambers and Lance Salway, in the September 1979 issue of *Signal*, seem to go out of their way to praise Judy Blume's virtues: "She can encapsulate an emotion or a perception in a single sentence that makes the reader know it for himself as well as knowing it for the character in the book". . . "She really does know how children feel and think and react". . . "I was quite bowled over by her expertise". . . Her "books deserve the same popularity here as they enjoy in the States." Admittedly *Signal* often has a tendency to praise American literature at the expense of English fiction (characterized as too "middle class" apparently, too "safe," too "conventional"), but its judgment on Judy Blume seems to imply that characterization, good English, narrative skill — indeed all the criteria a reviewer should use in assessing a book's merits — are no longer of any importance. And that psychological truth, especially in writing for children, is unimportant too — another "problem" in *Then Again, Maybe I Won't* is twelve-year-old Vic's developing sexuality; he's worried that he doesn't have wet dreams and the other fellows do — presumably what Judy Blume feels is the masculine

179

equivalent of having one's first period. Vic's feelings about wet dreams and Margaret's feelings about periods in *Are You There, God? It's Me, Margaret* are more or less identical, but these two bodily functions are profoundly different, psychologically, and Judy Blume is mistaken in leaving the reader with the impression that they are similar. That, and other elementary considerations — that writing about such topics so obsessively may cause hang-ups in the child reader where none existed previously — seem to escape the notice of her advocates.

In talking about the sexual development of young people Judy Blume is at her most insensitive, which is why *Forever* is easily her worst book. She has little idea, it seems, of what really occurs, emotionally, in adolescent sexual relationships, either in real life or in the teenage novel. Jessica Yates, writing in an earlier edition of *Signal*, talks of a kind of consensus arrived at by authors and publishers on the subject of how sexual relationships should be portrayed in novels for the young. The author should "examine either the procreational side of sex, or its emotional consequences (or both). This has led to a moral attitude which, while avoiding the tones of Victorian and Dickensian didacticism, nevertheless emphasizes the pains rather than the pleasures of sexual relationships, and declares that to embark on sex one must be on the way towards personal maturity and responsibility in dealing with other people." If she is right, then it seems to me that we are being a bit too cautious in some areas; I don't see why the teenage novel should necessarily examine the "procreational side of sex" nor dwell on "the pains rather than the pleasures of sexual relationships." I tend to agree with Norma Klein, who said in "Growing Up Human" that she would like to see teenage books which showed "young people having affairs which lead neither to abortion, pregnancy, or marriage, but possibly to pleasure and the complications ensuing from any close or loving relationship." She also mentioned other aspects of life the adolescent novel ought to consider, but which, all too often, it doesn't: "I would like a book in which one of the parents is homosexual and the child has to grapple with comprehending and coping with this. I would like books about interracial love affairs, which in a city like New York are not infrequent and not usually as horrendous and star-crossed as we've been led to believe. As a feminist, I would like, most of all, books about young girls discovering, not in the 'will I get invited to the junior prom?' sense, what it is to be young and female in this new and sometimes bewildering age of ours."

Judy Blume is not the only novelist who is offering the young poor value. It bothers me that Paul Zindel, for instance, suggests no palatable alternative to Yvette in *I Never Loved Your Mind*, so that Dewey Daniels can have some area of choice where girls are concerned, and that the emphasis in *My Darling, My Hamburger* is so much on the terrible things that may happen to teenage love affairs — rejection, unwanted pregnancy, abortion. There is, it's true, an alternative offered here in the relationship between Dennis and Maggie, but it's so anemic and unfulfilling that one may feel the message is that it's unsafe to venture into any kind of experience with the opposite sex. J. M. Couper, in *Looking for a Wave*, seems to me to be saying this even more explicitly: under the guise of a highly permissive viewpoint from the central character — twenty-year-old Mark, who, it is implied, knows *all* about girls, and through the use of a lot of impenetrably dense Australian slang (both of which are meant to seduce the young reader into thinking the writer is very much on his side) a solemn and didactic intention is revealed which boils down to "you must not do anything until you're married to the right sort of girl." Syphilis and gonorrhea are mentioned in this novel, but so vaguely and misleadingly that the adolescent reader is likely to be more scared than informed — an attitude to the subject that could easily lead to the spread of V.D.

rather than its reduction. A teenager could infer from this book that gonorrhea leads to the birth of children with deformed mouths, which is nonsense, and that people suffering from the disease are taken to hospital as in-patients. Furthermore, *I'll Get There: It Had Better Be Worth the Trip* by John Donovan suggests that homo-sexuality is so unacceptable socially and psychologically that any young homosexual will have his fears and worries increased rather than reduced, and the prejudice of the heterosexual against homosexuals is likely to be reinforced.

The whole area is beset with problems. Adults should be very sure they know what they are doing before they start writing about young love in novels intended for a teenage readership. The two most important things to avoid are, firstly, relying on their own memories, because everything — social behavior, sexual mores, language, re-lationships with parents and teachers — has changed out of all recognition; and, secondly, allowing their own prejudices and didactic intentions, conscious or un-conscious, to fill the pages, whether those feelings be in favor of keeping the young out of each other's beds, as in *Looking for a Wave*, or of getting them to leap in as quickly as possible, as in *Forever*. One turns back grate-fully to Jill Chaney. Or to Ursula Le Guin, for it is interesting to see how the greatest living exponent of the myth-and-legend story handles the teenage love affair: in *Very Far Away from Anywhere Else* she might almost be making an explicit criticism of books like *Forever*. She makes a surprising stand, as she does in the Earthsea trilogy, for intellectual elitism — not at all a fashionable thing to do — and her young couple, Natalie and Owen, as precocious in some ways as Ged or Tenar or Arren, come to the conclusion that they aren't old enough to cope with a full sexual relationship. Owen looks at the Judy-Blume-type adolescent world with a distinctly jaundiced eye:

You have to be with it. That's a peculiar phrase, you know? With it. With what? With them. With the others. All together. Safety in numbers. I'm not me. I'm a basketball color. I'm a popular kid. I'm my friends' friend. I'm a black leather growth on a Honda. I'm a member. I'm a teenager. You can't see me, all you can see is us. We're safe.

Surely all that's finest in all of us struggles to be what Owen wants to be — an individual, mature, and capable of choice — and what's timid, immature, and self-destructive in us wants to be what Kath and Michael are in *Forever*: conformist, safe, only capable of boasting that they're doing exactly what everybody else boasts of doing.

Ursula Le Guin one can read again and again. Not so Judy Blume. For me it isn't a question of forever or not: her novels don't even make a pleasurable one-night stand.

References

JUDY BLUME
> *Are You There, God? It's Me, Margaret* Bradbury 1970; Gollancz 1978
> *Then Again, Maybe I Won't* Bradbury 1971; Heinemann 1979
> *It's Not the End of the World* Bradbury 1972; Heinemann 1979
> *Tales of a Fourth Grade Nothing* Dutton 1972; Bodley Head 1979
> *Otherwise Known as Sheila the Great* Dutton 1972; Bodley Head 1979
> *Forever* Bradbury 1975; Gollancz 1976

NICHOLAS TUCKER
> review in the *Times Literary Supplement* of *Forever*

NANCY CHAMBERS AND LANCE SALWAY
> "Book Post" *Signal* September 1979

JESSICA YATES
> "Book Post Returns" *Signal* January 1979

CONSTANCE GREENE
I Know You, Al Viking 1975; Kestrel 1977

NORMA KLEIN
"Growing Up Human" in *Children's literature in
education* Summer 1977

PAUL ZINDEL
My Darling, My Hamburger Harper 1969; Bodley Head
1970
I Never Loved Your Mind Harper 1970; Bodley Head
1971

J. M. COUPER
Looking for a Wave Bodley Head 1973; Bradbury 1975

JOHN DONOVAN
I'll Get There: It Had Better Be Worth the Trip
Harper 1969; Macdonald 1970

URSULA K. LE GUIN
Very Far Away from Anywhere Else Atheneum 1976;
Gollancz 1976 (as *A Very Long Way from Anywhere
Else*)
A Wizard of Earthsea Parnassus 1968; Gollancz 1971
The Tombs of Atuan Atheneum 1971; Gollancz 1972
The Farthest Shore Atheneum 1972; Gollancz 1973

Time Present
and Time Past

◆

PENELOPE LIVELY

"IT IS THE PERCEPTION, often startling, that places have a past, that they are now but also then, and that if peopled now, they were peopled then." This quotation, from Penelope Lively's article "Children and Memory," well illustrates the major preoccupation of her novels; it is a theme that occurs and recurs, almost obsessively, in all her books from *Astercote* to *The Voyage of QV 66*. It is a perception, she says, that is "a step out of the child's self-preoccupation"; it is "a step towards maturity." Nearly all her novels have, as their main characters, children who are making that step towards maturity.

Penelope Lively would have to write only slightly differently to find herself labeled by those people who need to pigeonhole books into categories as an historical novelist for children and to find herself compared with Rosemary Sutcliff, Henry Treece, or other writers of that genre. After all, her interests seem to be historical — the Black Death, Morgan le Fay, seventeenth-century ghosts, ancient ritual dances of the Exmoor area. None of her books, of course, is set in the period of any of these; they are set firmly in the twentieth century; and the reader is constantly made aware of this fact by references to supermarkets, plans for building motorways, rows of council houses. "Places . . . are now but also then." In her ◆ 185 concern for what is happening now and how the past helps to shape the present, Penelope Lively differs from

the historical novelist who is more interested, perhaps ex-
clusively interested, in what happened "then." She is
nearer to the writer of fantasy, the writer who uses
parallel stories of past and present — such as Lucy Boston
in *The Children of Green Knowe* or, less obviously perhaps, John Christopher, who, in *The White Mountains*
and *The Guardians*, uses a real past and a fantasy future
to meditate on the problems of the present — as she does
herself in *The Voyage of QV 66*.

But these comparisons are inexact; though there is a
similar feeling, as in Lucy Boston's work, of the influence
of place and history in shaping the lives of those who
people her books, there is not the sense of displacement,
of disorientation, that so interests Lucy Boston — Ping, the
Chinese boy, and Hanno, the gorilla, set in utterly alien
environments. Much luckier, much more capable of en-
richment, are the children in Penelope Lively's novels.
Even if those children come originally from other places
and their middle-class backgrounds mean some loss of
roots, their own lives are firmly involved in the community: the large sprawling Midlands villages with their
sense of the past — ancient field-patterns and parish
registers — and with their thriving present — new housing
estates and traffic problems. And unlike John Christopher,
Penelope Lively is not asking what kind of society do
we wish to live in, how do we wish to develop; society
to her evolves from a slow, natural growth and is not
capable of violent change, nor does it need such change.
The past is never made to seem worse than the present,
nor better — Chipping Ledbury must cope with the problems caused by motorway planners that threaten to destroy
it, just as Astercote had to cope with the Black Death.
The Harrison family, in *The Ghost of Thomas Kempe*,
has all the advantages of the comforts of modern living
combined with a rewarding sense of the past; but not so
for Betsy Tranter, in *Astercote*, who has all the dis-
advantages of such a combination.

Comparisons with other authors lead nowhere when writing about Penelope Lively. There may be a hint of Virginia Woolf, even of Philippa Pearce, in *The House in Norham Gardens*, only because of a slight similarity in language; there may be a hint of Penelope Farmer in *The Wild Hunt of the Ghost Hounds*, but only because of a likeness in landscape. What Penelope Lively has achieved in her novels is something unique, a kind of book that is neither history nor fantasy but has something of both, and that cannot be labeled conveniently — a book where the power of place is a stronger force than most of the characters, where "history is now."

How has she managed to achieve such an individual niche in the very cluttered world of children's books, where works of fantasy and history come ten a penny? It is obvious from her first novel *Astercote* that, despite its faults, here is a writer who is capable of putting together an exciting narrative, one in which the pace is exactly right and which, if nothing else, will keep the reader turning the pages to see what happens. This is no achievement to be scorned; unfolding a story bit by bit is to most writers a much more difficult task than composing a poetic piece about a sunset. *Astercote* seems immediately different from most other books. Goacher, one feels, is a character who could have been conceived by no other writer; and who else would posit a suggestion — one that the reader is made to take seriously — that the theft of Astercote's chalice could actually lead to a possibility of an outbreak of bubonic plague?

> Piecing together what he had said they began to make sense of the story. After the last of the villagers had died someone — someone who Goacher could not name but sometimes referred to confusingly as "us" or "we" — had taken the chalice from the church and hidden it. Hidden it because it belonged to Astercote and in Astercote it should remain. And because, or so they began to understand from Goacher's vague, confused talk,

♦ 187

because whoever took it had come to believe that it enshrined something precious, something magical, that would prevent such a catastrophe ever happening again.

There are faults in the writing: Some of the characterization, particularly that of the district nurse, is thin and unconvincing; and there seems to be a curious infirmity of purpose at one important point in the novel, as if the author had not really made up her mind which way the book was going to develop — will the plague *really* return? The reader is a little disappointed that it does not: He is left with a feeling that the author has avoided that possibility because it was, at that point, beyond her power to deal with.

Most of these awkwardnesses are ironed out in the next two books, *The Whispering Knights* and *The Wild Hunt of the Ghost Hounds*. Both deal with similar themes and are structurally similar to *Astercote*. The children, however, are much more sharply individualized in *The Whispering Knights* than in *Astercote*; and the minor characters in *The Wild Hunt of the Ghost Hounds* are treated ironically — a very successful excursion into satirical social observation and a way of looking at character that Penelope Lively does not use again until *A Stitch in Time*:

> The woman who opened the door was carelessly, even shabbily, dressed. A crucial button was missing from her blouse, her skirt was faded and pinned where the zip had broken. This seemed to indicate self-confidence rather than poverty, and matched the appearance of the furnishings visible behind her: battered, but originally expensive. She shared with the house, the garden, the stables beyond, an appearance of needing to make no unnecessary statements about a position in the world.

Irony would have improved *Astercote*.

188 ♦ In *The Whispering Knights* Morgan le Fay affects the lives of Susie, Martha, and William; and in *The Wild Hunt* the revival of the horn dance affects Lucy and

Kester more than the stolen chalice affects Mair and Peter in *Astercote*. The difference between these two books and *Astercote* is that the evil caused by a silly meddling with the past is a real evil, not an imaginary one. As a result, there is no slackening of the narrative tension in the last stages of *The Wild Hunt* or *The Whispering Knights*; on the contrary, the concluding chapters contain the most exciting writing of the books — where the struggle between good and evil reaches its climax:

> They lay face down in the grass, not daring to move or look up, and around and above them the battle roared. There was the terrible crash of stone against stone, the whistle of steel in the air, the screech of steel on stone, and the piercing shrieks of Morgan's fury and frustration. And above it all the thunder played out its own battle. Once Martha dared to roll over a little and look up, and it seemed to her that the whole sky was in a ferment, and that the flowing shapes of the clouds were the shapes of some strange monstrous chase that raged back and forth above the valley, and then she glimpsed another flying shape, and felt the awesome movement of the Stones.

In *The Whispering Knights*, there are hints in the character of Martha that Penelope Lively is beginning to be interested in children who are not wholly uncomplicated and nice. And in *The Wild Hunt* there is a very odd and unusual, but sympathetic character, Kester: a child who deliberately invites persecution; in Kester there is something more complex than what she had achieved before — a convincing mixture of contradictions.

If the first three novels are similar in theme and structure, their successors are not only very different, but different from each other in these respects, though the preoccupations with "places . . . are now but also then" and with how it was for the people "then" remain. *The Driftway*, Penelope Lively says in "Children and Memory" "was an attempt to write about the jolt given to a child's self-absorption by an imaginative involvement with other people's lives. . . I wanted to use landscape as a channel for historical memory – a road, in fact, a perfectly ordinary road, B4525 from Banbury to Northampton, but a road that is very ancient and seemed to lend itself perfectly to a double symbolism." The road actually becomes the central character of the book rather than the boy, Paul, who is traveling on it, and it is used to hang somewhat loosely together various self-contained stories set in the past: the adventures, for example, of an eighteenth-century highwayman and a soldier escaping from a battle in the Civil War. It is probably the least successful of Penelope Lively's books, the only one which readers consistently say is dull. There is no loss in the quality of her writing ability; indeed there are passages, notably of landscape description, that are finer than anything she had previously done:

> As the brilliance of the day began to ebb away the countryside had a tired, worn look, as though the luxuriance of summer had drained it, leaving the gold and copper flaming in the hedges and trees as a last grand gesture: there was already a hint of winter in the bleached grasses that lined the road and the naked fields, patterned with the swirling curves of the plough.

But the book is shapeless. It seems to be the length it is because that is the standard length required by publishers. It could have been longer (a few more historical episodes inserted would not seem out of place), or shorter (a few of these episodes less and the reader would not notice anything missing). Old Bill, the cart-driver, is a totally unconvincing rustic, made of sentimental clichés about rural characters. The predicament of the central figure, Paul – who is running away from home because he cannot face up to the implications of his father's second marriage – remains curiously unfelt. The reader is never allowed to come fully to terms with the situation: Paul's father and stepmother remain outside the narrative and are only present in Paul's thoughts. So the reader is asked to share a vague emotive identification with Paul without enough information to go on.

Why does *The Driftway* fail so badly? Largely because the author has abandoned the technique she had mastered so ably — telling in a tight, exciting manner a highly readable narrative that has a beginning, a middle, and an end — and has substituted an experimental, impressionistic framework she does not know how to handle. In *The Ghost of Thomas Kempe*, which deservedly won the Carnegie Medal in 1973, she returned, fortunately, to the business of telling a story — with triumphant success. *Thomas Kempe* is about a poltergeist, an unsuccessful ghost who begs to be allowed to return to his own time and place. *The Wild Hunt of the Ghost Hounds* had shown how well Penelope Lively could write, if only fleetingly, in a comic vein; *Thomas Kempe* is a comedy from beginning to end and has a lightness of touch that never fails. Not only is the poor poltergeist a figure of fun, but Aunt Fanny's journal is a magnificent pastiche of a Victorian diary-writer. (One grumble: Would such a masterpiece have ever been thrown out onto a bonfire?)

> We are most agreeably busy. There is never a dull moment! Never a day goes by but the dear boy produces some new scheme for our entertainment. I had quite forgot what a variety of diversions the young have at their disposal. And I in my turn have done a little to instruct Arnold in the domestic arts for the dear boy being of an enquiring mind is not averse to learn how his favourite delicacies are made. He can make a passably good pie and also bake the plum and spice cakes of which he is so very fond.

And James, the central character — a sound, solid, boy-like boy — is just a bit larger than life, not exaggerated enough to be a caricature, but a little like Tom Sawyer. He fits perfectly into the world of this novel. Parents play a larger part in this book than in the previous three;

191

quite correctly, for the absence of parents in many children's books is often self-indulgence on the writer's part. Who, if not parents, play the largest role in a child's life? So here are Mr. and Mrs. Harrison, amusing and uncomprehending, so busily engaged in the tasks of earning a living or doing the housework that they cannot possibly begin to understand the fantastic or the supernatural, cannot even allow that they may exist. Poor James has to battle with Thomas Kempe alone.

The Ghost of Thomas Kempe is perhaps the first of Penelope Lively's novels in which the reader feels that the author is completely sure of her own abilities, and the writing has a positiveness that derives from the author's pleasure in her awareness of these abilities. Certainly it was her finest book so far, and armed with this new-found authority, she went on to deal with a more complex analysis, in *The House in Norham Gardens*, of the same themes that have always preoccupied her. The prose has a poetic, luminous quality that is a sheer delight; like Philippa Pearce's *The Children of the House*, it is a prose poem from beginning to end.

> And the snow fell. Indiscriminately, blotting out grass and pavements and road alike so that by evening the houses stood in a strange, undefined landscape neither town nor country. Cars were silenced and slowed, creeping past with diffidence, as though perhaps they had no business here. With darkness came a deep silence. Clare, lying in bed, awake in dark reaches of the night, strained for sounds and heard nothing. She could have been deaf, enclosed within her own mind and body. She had to get up and open the window to reassure herself. Somewhere, a car banged and people shouted to one another. She went back to bed again.

This is a far cry from the prose of *Astercote*, which was competent but flat, unmemorable.

Adults become even more important in *Norham Gardens* than in *Thomas Kempe*. Aunt Anne and Aunt

Susan are observed by both Clare and the author: difficult, eccentric, very old, wrapped in a way of life that has long since ceased to exist, only vaguely aware of the hardships they cause Clare, yet credible and sympathetic. Penelope Lively says "I think that for children an important moment of perception is when they see other people as not necessarily frozen at a moment in time — now — but as extended backwards. Parents as once children, grandparents as once young men and women. Themselves as potentially someone different." The emphasis in *Norham Gardens* lies not so much on "places . . . are now but also then" but on people who are now but also then. Not that place is neglected. The decaying Victorian suburbs of Oxford — with their grandiose houses that are symbols of an age of greater certainties than ours, crumbling or split up into flats, their gardens filled with weeds and students' bicycles — are created with great lovingness and care. But Aunt Anne and Aunt Susan are *people* from history and also of now, and this theme beguiles both the reader and Clare into an awareness that the hardships of her existence are mitigated by imaginative rewards denied to most children. "We are none of us 'the young,' or 'the middle-aged,' or 'the old.' We are all of these things. To allow children to think otherwise is to encourage a disability — a disability both of awareness and of communication."

The house is now and then; so are the aunts; and so, as a result, the element of fantasy in this novel is less strong than in any other of Penelope Lively's previous books, except perhaps for *Astercote*. Indeed it might have been dispensed with altogether; not that one wishes it were not there — for the fusion of the theme with the quest of the brown men of New Guinea for their lost shield is highly successful. In fact, the fantasy element shows another perspective of history and memory and their relationship to the present — not only are people and places of now and then, but also objects, even when they are torn out of their environment and taken into other, incongruous situations where they apparently have no meaning.

After *The House in Norham Gardens*, the complete absence of fantasy in *Going Back* comes as no surprise; and in its successor, *A Stitch in Time*, it is firmly established as the product of a lonely child's overactive imagination, not as a force to be reckoned with in its own right. Both books are still concerned, however, with past and present; in *Going Back* Jane's comfortable married middle age is compared with her childhood in the Second World War, and in *A Stitch in Time*, Maria, on holiday in Lyme Regis in an old house that has hardly changed in a hundred years, becomes so involved with thinking about a Victorian girl who lived there that she imagines she is going to suffer the same supposed fate, death in a landslide. *Going Back* is not entirely satisfactory. Its opening chapter — Jane revisiting the village in Somerset where she was brought up — attempts a similar kind of poetic prose-style to that of *The House in Norham Gardens*, but it doesn't work so well: the place hasn't fired the writer's imagination quite so vividly. The children's father is an unconvincing figure: one could understand his being heavy-handed and insensitive, but he is so repellent, so totally nasty, that the reader cannot believe in him as a probability. The other characters, however, are excellent, and the narrative, after an unusually slow start, holds the reader in its spell. The strange new aspects of life in war-time, both pleasant and unpleasant, are emphasized in detail, and particularly good is the initial lack of comprehension with which Jane and her brother greet things entirely out of the ordinary:

> "What's a land-girl?" said Edward, and Betty flashing past with table-lamps and pillow-cases, snapped, "You'll find out soon enough."
> We knew our Hans Andersen and our *Tales of Ancient Greece*. Like water-nymphs, we decided, or

tree-spirits. Elemental, elusive creatures. We waited, hopefully, for them to appear.

Jane, throwing a quoit, chants "Immunization and evacuation and mobilization *and* immunization and evacuation and mobilization." She does not know what the words mean, but "they are good words," she says. " 'Conscription,' I yell at the sky, and miss the quoit again." It was indeed very like that for great numbers of English children. And, most interestingly, in *Going Back*, there are signs that Penelope Lively has growing doubts about the kind of material she has, since *Astercote*, chosen to use:

> People's lives tell a story, I thought once: and then, and next, and then. . . But they don't. Nothing so simple. If it's a story at all, then there are two of them, running side by side. What actually happened, and what we remember. Which is more important, I wonder?

A Stitch in Time is a perfect illustration of those doubts, distinguishing between what actually happened to Harriet (nothing very much) and what Maria imagines happened to her (a melodramatic death). Yet the influence of the past on the present is seen as enormous, even though the author seems to be saying that we can never exactly realize what it was like to be living in a bygone age. This is well conveyed in the person of the landlady, Mrs. Shand, who was a child in late Victorian times, and, surrounded as she is by relics of the past, she is not the girl she was then; she's a rather sharp-tongued old woman with a faulty understanding of children, and her interest in the past is little more than a sentimental wish to keep family mementoes. Maria looks in her face "for the shadow of this other person she must once have been, and could not find it." *A Stitch in Time* is probably Penelope Lively's most important and memorable book. Not only is its exploration of the significance of history and memory more profound than in any other of her novels, but the unfolding of the story is very fine, and the power of place has rarely been better done in a children's novel.

Lyme Regis is a town soaked in history, and along with its unpredictable landslides it is famous for its fossils and pre-history; but it's also a modern seaside resort: she manages to suggest that like people it has layers, now and then. The book also shows Penelope Lively's gifts as a humorist — the social comedy, contrasting two completely different families, one noisy, slapdash, and chaotic, the other so organized that all spontaneous life has been crushed out of it, is extremely well handled. She has little good to say about the stultifying Fosters:

> Aunt Ruth, Maria had noticed before, was a person who felt unsafe if detached too long from London. She plunged beyond it, briefly, rather as a nervous swimmer plunges into the sea with head always turned towards the shore.

Their interest in the past is shallow and frivolous:

> She was herself something of an expert on stately homes. Mr and Mrs Foster enjoyed a drive to such places on a Sunday afternoon: it got you out of London, you saw the countryside (conveniently displayed, neither muddy nor cold, on the other side of the car windows) and you were taking an interest in history. Such outings could do you nothing but good.

No wonder Maria, their only child, is so bored and lonely that she is given to talking aloud to cats and petrol-pumps and clocks. But she's a girl of spirit, if somewhat repressed, and has some moments of splendid indignation. Looking at a notice that says "No Children or Dogs," she's able to tell herself

> There are, after all, both children and dogs — lots of them, all over the place. So there's nothing to be done about it. You might as well say No Rain or Earthquakes.

The change in Penelope Lively's attitude to the past is an important development. Mrs. Shand says:

> "Things always could have been otherwise. The fact of the matter is that they are not. What has been,

has been. What is, is." She stabbed the needle confidently into the brown canvas.

"I suppose so," said Maria. "But it's a very difficult thing to get used to."

"One does eventually," said Mrs Shand, "there being no other choice."

She chose to set her most recent novel, *The Voyage of QV 66*, in the future, which, after the questions raised in *A Stitch in Time*, is quite logical; she clearly felt a strong need to take a very different look at the themes that have preoccupied her until now. So this story is all fantasy and no history. Its protagonists are talking animals who have survived a disastrous flood that has destroyed the whole of mankind. It's a very amusing tale, but it's cautious and experimental, its characters too predictable, incapable of giving the reader any sense of surprise. It was reviewed almost ecstatically in England, but it doesn't begin to measure up to *A Stitch in Time*. No matter; an author making such a radical change of direction as Penelope Lively does here is unlikely to write a masterpiece at once. Or is it a dead end? It's not easy to predict her next move. Yet there are some absorbing passages in *The Voyage of QV 66*, particularly when the animals are meditating on the nature of men and their achievements. Its conclusions are somber: man was a pretty nasty piece of work on the whole, and there is a danger that his mistakes will be repeated. Already the dogs are beginning to organize themselves into fascist-like packs, and the monkeys are, in an extremely primitive way, inventing machines. Good, too, is the author's liberal attitude to outsiders and misfits — the book expresses a sense of outrage that nonconformists must automatically be persecuted or eliminated.

Children "can't yet place themselves in a wider framework of time and space than *today* and *here*," Penelope Lively wrote in "Children and Memory": "But they have to, if they are not to grow up enclosed in their own personalities. Perhaps books can help, just a little." Her most recent work seems to be suggesting that it is a very hard task indeed. Maria's experiences in *A Stitch in Time* may have prevented her from being enclosed in *her* own personality, but no such optimism pervades *The Voyage of QV 66*. Penelope Lively's next novel — if in fact she hasn't written herself out as far as children's books are concerned — will be different again. One awaits it eagerly; she's undoubtedly the most interesting author of children's fiction to have emerged in the nineteen-seventies.

References

PENELOPE LIVELY
Astercote Heinemann 1970; Dutton 1971
The Whispering Knights Heinemann 1971; Dutton 1976
The Wild Hunt of Hagworthy Heinemann 1971; Dutton 1972 (as *The Wild Hunt of the Ghost Hounds*)
The Driftway Heinemann 1972; Dutton 1973
The Ghost of Thomas Kempe Heinemann 1973; Dutton 1973
The House in Norham Gardens Heinemann 1974; Dutton 1974
Going Back Heinemann 1975; Dutton 1975
A Stitch in Time Heinemann 1976; Dutton 1976
The Voyage of QV 66 Heinemann 1978; Dutton 1979
"Children and Memory" *The Horn Book Magazine*, August 1973

LUCY BOSTON
The Children of Green Knowe Faber 1954; Harcourt 1967

BRIAN FAIRFAX-LUCY AND PHILIPPA PEARCE
The Children of the House Longman 1968; Lippincott 1968

JOHN CHRISTOPHER
The White Mountains Hamish Hamilton 1967; Macmillan, New York, 1967
The Guardians Hamish Hamilton 1970; Macmillan, New York, 1970

Index

Permission Acknowledgments

Pages 204 to 211 constitute an extension of the copyright page. Permission to quote from the text of copyrighted works is gratefully acknowledged to the following:

AGATHON PRESS, INC.

Excerpts from essays by David Rees, which appeared in *Children's literature in education*: "The Novels of Philippa Pearce" March 1971, © 1971 *Children's literature in education*; "A Plea for Jill Chaney" Summer 1977, © 1977 APS Publications, Inc., "The Colour of Skin: James Vance Marshall" Summer 1980, © 1980 APS Publications, Inc.

ATHENEUM PUBLISHERS

Excerpts from *A Castle of Bone* © 1972 by Penelope Farmer, *William and Mary* © 1974 by Penelope Farmer, and *Year King* © 1977 by Penelope Farmer, all by Penelope Farmer, are reprinted courtesy of Atheneum Publishers.

Excerpts from *The Dragon in the Ghetto Caper* © 1974 by E. L. Konigsburg, *From the Mixed-up Files of Mrs. Basil E. Frankweiler* © 1967 by E. L. Konigsburg, (*George*) © 1978 by E. L. Konigsburg, and *Jennifer, Hecate, Macbeth, William McKinley, and me, Elizabeth* © 1967 by E. L. Konigsburg, all by E. L. Konigsburg, are reprinted courtesy of Atheneum Publishers.

Excerpts from *The Farthest Shore* © 1972 by Ursula K. Le Guin, *The Tombs of Atuan* © 1971 by Ursula K. Le Guin, *Very Far Away from Anywhere Else* © 1976 by Ursula K. Le Guin, all by Ursula K. Le Guin, are reprinted courtesy of Atheneum Publishers.

THE BODLEY HEAD

Excerpts from *Confessions of a Teenage Baboon* Copyright © 1977 by Zindel Productions Incorporated, *I Never Loved Your Mind* Copyright © 1970 by Paul Zindel, and *The Pigman* Copyright © 1968 by Paul Zindel, all by Paul Zindel, are reprinted by permission of The Bodley Head.

right, 1952, by E. B. White, Text copyright renewed ©
1980 by E. B. White, are reprinted by permission of
Harper & Row, Publishers, Inc.

Excerpts from *Confessions of a Teenage Baboon* by Paul
Zindel, Copyright © 1977 by Zindel Productions In-
corporated, reprinted by courtesy of Harper & Row,
Publishers, Inc; excerpt from *I Never Loved Your
Mind*: A Novel by Paul Zindel, Copyright © 1970 by
Paul Zindel, reprinted by courtesy of Harper & Row,
Publishers, Inc.; excerpt from *The Pigman*: A Novel by
Paul Zindel, Copyright © 1968 by Paul Zindel, reprinted
by permission of Harper & Row, Publishers, Inc.

Excerpts from *Jazz Country* by Nat Hentoff. Copyright © 1965 by Nat Hentoff. Reprinted by courtesy of
Harper & Row, Publishers, Inc.

WILLIAM HEINEMANN LTD.

Excerpts from *Astercote*, Copyright © 1970 by Penelope
Lively, *The Driftway*, Copyright © 1972 by Penelope
Lively, *The Ghost of Thomas Kempe*, Text copyright
© 1973 by Penelope Lively, *Going Back*, Copyright ©
1975 by Penelope Lively, *The House in Norham Gar-
dens*, Copyright © 1974 by Penelope Lively, *A Stitch in
Time*, Copyright © 1976 by Penelope Lively, *The
Whispering Knights*, Text copyright © 1971 by Penelope
Lively, *The Wild Hunt of Hagworthy*, Copyright ©
Penelope Lively 1971, all by Penelope Lively, are re-
printed by courtesy of William Heinemann Ltd.

Excerpts from *It's Not the End of the World*, Copy-
right © 1972 by Judy Blume, and *Then Again Maybe I
Won't*, Copyright © 1971 by Judy Blume, both by Judy
Blume, are reprinted courtesy of William Heinemann
Ltd.

Excerpts from *A Taste of Blackberries* by Doris
Buchanan Smith, Copyright © 1973 by Doris Buchanan
Smith, are reprinted courtesy of William Heinemann
208   ♦   Ltd.

THE HORN BOOK, INC.

Excerpts from "Time Present and Time Past: Penelope

Paula Fox, *The Slave Dancer*, Copyright © 1973 by Paula Fox, *The Stone-Faced Boy*, Copyright © 1968 by Paula Fox, all by Paula Fox, reprinted by courtesy of Macmillan, London and Basingstoke.

Excerpts from *The Diddakoi* by Rumer Godden, Copyright © 1972 by Rumer Productions Ltd., reprinted by courtesy of Macmillan, London and Basingstoke.
Excerpts from *The Dragon in the Ghetto Caper*, Copyright © 1974 by E. L. Konigsburg, *(George)*, Copyright ©1970 by E. L. Konigsburg, *Jennifer, Hecate, Macbeth and Me*, Copyright © 1967 by E. L. Konigsburg, *The Mixed-up Files of Mrs. Basil E. Frankweiler*, Copyright © 1967 by E. L. Konigsburg, all by E. L. Konigsburg, are reprinted by permission of Macmillan, London and Basingstoke.

Excerpts from *The Emperor's Winding Sheet*, Copyright © 1974 by Jill Paton Walsh, *Fireweed*, Copyright © 1969 by Jill Paton Walsh, and *Hengest's Tale*, © G. Paton Walsh 1966, all by Jill Paton Walsh, are reprinted courtesy of Macmillan, London and Basingstoke.

WILLIAM MORROW & COMPANY, INC.
Excerpts from *Ramona and Her Father*, Copyright © 1975, 1977 by Beverly Cleary, and *Ramona the Pest*, Copyright © 1968 by Beverly Cleary, both by Beverly Cleary, are reprinted by courtesy of William Morrow & Company, Inc.

Excerpts from *Walkabout* by James Vance Marshall, Copyright © 1959 by James Vance Marshall. Revised edition Copyright © 1971 by William Morrow and Company, Inc., is reprinted by courtesy of William Morrow and Company, Inc.

OXFORD UNIVERSITY PRESS
Excerpts from *Minnow on the Say* by A. Philippa Pearce (1955) and *Tom's Midnight Garden* by A. Philippa Pearce © Oxford University Press 1958, reprinted by permission of Oxford University Press.

PANTHEON BOOKS, INC.
Excerpts from *After the First Death*, Copyright © 1979